SUPERINTENDENT EVALUATION HANDBOOK

Michael F. DiPaola
James H. Stronge

A SCARECROWEDUCATION BOOK

Published in partnership with the
American Association of School Administrators
The Scarecrow Press, Inc.
Lanham, Maryland, and Oxford
2003

A SCARECROWEDUCATION BOOK
Published in partnership with
the American Association of School Administrators

Published in the United States of America
by Scarecrow Press, Inc.
A Member of the Rowman & Littlefield Publishing Group
4720 Boston Way, Lanham, Maryland 20706
www.scarecroweducation.com

PO Box 317
Oxford
OX2 9RU, UK

Copyright © 2003 by Michael F. DiPaola and James H. Stronge

British Library Cataloguing in Publication Information Available

Library of Congress Cataloging-in-Publication Data
DiPaola, Michael F., 1947–
  Superintendent evaluation handbook / Michael F. DiPaola, James H. Stronge.
    p. cm.
  "A ScarecrowEducation book."
  Includes bibliographical references (p.　) and index.
  ISBN 0-8108-4607-1 (pbk. : alk. paper)
  1. School superintendents—Rating of—United States—Handbooks, manuals,
  etc. I. Stronge, James H. II. Title.
  LB2831.762.D56 2003
  371.2'011—dc21   2002012348

In memory of Michael A. and Carmela DiPaola, loving and supportive parents. Dedicated to Valerie, my love and soulmate.

—Michael

Dedicated to Harold and Birdie Stronge, wonderful parents.

—James

CONTENTS

ILLUSTRATIONS

❶

SUPERINTENDENT EVALUATION: GETTING STARTED

A conceptually sound and properly implemented evaluation system for the superintendent is a vital component of an effective school system. Regardless of how well educational programs may be designed, the programs are only as effective as the people who implement and support them. Thus, a rational relationship exists between personnel and programs: effective people ensure effective programs. If program effectiveness is important and if personnel are necessary for effective programming, then a conceptually sound and properly implemented evaluation system for all employees, including the superintendent, is essential.

The purpose of the *Superintendent Evaluation Handbook* is to explore the important issue of evaluation for the superintendent, addressing the aspects of that process that make it unique. We begin with this introductory chapter in which we address the questions of

- Why is superintendent evaluation an important issue?
- What particular challenges are posed by superintendent evaluation?
- What are criteria for superintendent evaluation?

Finally, we conclude with a brief description of how the *Superintendent Evaluation Handbook* is organized.

WHY IS SUPERINTENDENT EVALUATION
AN IMPORTANT ISSUE?

Despite the fact that proper evaluation of the superintendent of schools is fundamentally important, this aspect of performance evaluation has too frequently been neglected. Personnel evaluations in education historically have focused primarily on classroom teachers and, in more recent years, on principals, counselors, and other building-based personnel. In 1980, the American Association of School Administrators (AASA) and the National School Boards Association (NSBA) issued a joint statement calling for formal evaluations of superintendents (AASA, 1980), yet in the intervening years little systemic progress has been made. While these positions are vital to school success, we can no longer afford to overlook the performance evaluation of the school system's CEO—the superintendent.

Whether we are discussing the evaluation of the superintendent, the classroom teacher, or another position, the need is basic: a thoughtful, thorough, and fair evaluation based on performance and designed to encourage improvement in both the person being evaluated and the school. Nonetheless, the job of the superintendent and, consequently, her or his evaluation are unique within the school system.

Regarding the work of the superintendent, the position is an amalgam of

- strategic planner,
- leader,
- cheerleader,
- organizational manager,
- fiscal officer,
- diplomat,
- politician, and
- other equally important roles.

In essence, the superintendent personifies the aspirations and responsibilities of the entire organization. On the other hand, when it comes to performance assessment, the superintendent's evaluation is too frequently conducted through a highly informal process based more on impressions than real data (Peterson, 1989). Moreover, she or he is the only employee in the entire organization who is supervised by multiple evaluators, all of whom typically are community members untrained in the evaluation of professional educators. The success of the superintendent and, ultimately, the success of the school system are inextricably tied. If the superintendent of schools is to receive a fair evaluation, and if the evaluation is to contribute to her or his success and to the overall effectiveness of the school system as a whole, then special consideration must be given to designing, developing, and implementing a comprehensive and quality performance evaluation system.

WHAT PARTICULAR CHALLENGES ARE POSED BY SUPERINTENDENT EVALUATION?

Designing and implementing a sound performance evaluation system for the superintendent is a comprehensive and complex undertaking that we explore in more depth in subsequent chapters. A brief review of three of the more practical problems that face boards of education in implementing an evaluation system appropriate for the superintendent serves as a foundation for further discussion

- using multiple evaluators,
- clarifying performance expectations, and
- documenting performance.

Multiple Evaluators: Multiple Expectations

One of the factors that makes the evaluation of the superintendent unique is the lack of a single supervisor determining performance expectations. Typically, the superintendent is evaluated by all members of the board, most of whom are lay members of the community who have uneven—or a lack of—training in performance evaluation (MacPhail-Wilcox & Forbes, 1990). Consequently, when five, seven, or nine members of the school board evaluate the superintendent, the resulting evaluation can be a conglomerate of conflicting perspectives—both in terms of expectations and performance. With this practice, one of two approaches frequently emerges

1. The diverse opinions regarding the superintendent's performance get bandied about by the board members until a general consensus, an averaging of the varied opinions, or a compromise emerges.
2. The school board simply compiles all of the ratings and comments of individual board members and presents the composite list to the superintendent as the final evaluation.

Neither process serves the superintendent, the board, or the community well. With the first approach—evaluation by averaging—the feedback is too frequently general in nature and lacking in specificity. In the second approach—evaluation by composite—the feedback is too specific, offering conflicting advice and directives. Both methods result in an evaluation that is a general "feel good" approach when things are perceived to be going well, or that can result in acrimony among the board members and between the board and the superintendent when things are not going well. Thus, both of these approaches are counterproductive to the success of the board, the superintendent, and, ultimately, the primary clients of the school system—the students.

Performance Expectations

Another problem often plaguing the superintendent evaluation process is the absence of clearly defined job expectations and performance goals. For a new superintendent, often the assumption is that the selection process clarified the expectations; for a continuing superintendent, a general understanding based on past practice frequently is used. Few superintendents receive suggestions for improvement during an evaluation and meaningful evaluations should address both strengths and weaknesses (Candoli, Cullen, & Stufflebeam, 1997). A better process for both the new and the continuing superintendent is to jointly establish with the board clear and specific goals for the organization and the expectations of the superintendent in fulfilling those goals (Schaffer, 1999). By discussing and collaboratively establishing mutually agreeable organizational goals and performance targets, the job of the superintendent can more readily be translated into job responsibilities with appropriate performance indicators and standards for job performance. This collaborative process clearly requires input from both the school board and the superintendent, who ultimately is responsible for carrying out the daily performance of job expectations. Only by a joint process of defining responsibilities and standards of performance can there be clear direction for the school system, the evaluation process, and the superintendent being evaluated.

Documentation of Performance

Documenting the superintendent's job performance should also be considered a collaborative process, with both the board and the superintendent gathering and assessing performance data. However, the critical issue is the need to rely on tangible, objective ways of knowing how well the superintendent performs. When the superintendent's evaluation is based merely on supposition drawn from informal sources, the evidence upon which decisions are made is superficial.

An informal process for documenting performance can easily result in numerous problems including

- perceptions skewed by a few vocal advocates or complainants;
- performance reviews based on anecdotal, partial evidence;
- evaluations unrelated to measures of success or achievement of organizational goals;
- a false sense of security regarding progress;
- decisions uninformed by results; and
- the absence of clear direction for continuous improvement and future direction.

Rather than rely on poor or partial evidence for documenting performance, we advocate a system that builds upon multiple sources of performance evidence, including goal accomplishment, self-assessment, informal observation, client feedback, and analysis of artifacts. The use of multiple data sources such as these can more accurately reflect the multifaceted job dimensions of the superintendent's role and success in fulfilling that role.

WHAT ARE CRITERIA FOR
SUPERINTENDENT EVALUATION?

To begin, any personnel evaluation system should properly address the standards developed by the Joint Committee on Standards for Educational Evaluation (1988): propriety, utility, feasibility, and accuracy. Although there may be unique aspects to the nature of the superintendent's role, the position has in common with all educational personnel the need for fair, job-relevant, and meaningful evaluations. Unfortunately, as with teachers and administrators, superintendents have suffered from numerous systemic problems with the state-of-the-art of personnel evaluation (Stronge, at press). The Joint Committee on Standards for Educational Evaluation (1988) stated that personnel evaluation has been ineffectively conducted in educational organizations, despite the centrality of the process.

Dominant criticisms of personnel evaluation practices include

- lack of constructive feedback,
- failure to recognize and reinforce outstanding service, and
- dividing rather than unifying collective efforts to educate students.

For evaluation to be beneficial to the superintendent and the school system, traditional problems such as those noted above must be resolved. One ready solution is to develop and implement performance evaluation systems that adhere to the Personnel Evaluation Standards. A brief overview of how the four basic standards can be incorporated into superintendent evaluation is provided in Figure 1.1. A detailed discussion of each of the four sets of standards follows.

Propriety Standards

Propriety Standards "require that evaluations be conducted legally, ethically, and with due regard for the welfare of evaluatees and clients of the evaluations" (Joint Committee, 1988, p. 21). Ultimately the superintendent's evaluation should establish a system that directly supports the primary principle—that schools exist to serve students. For ease of reference, a number indicating the specific standard follows the

Figure 1.1. Application of Personnel Evaluation Standards to Superintendent Evaluation

Standards	Description of the Standards	Application to Superintendent Evaluation
Propriety Standards ...	"require that evaluations be conducted legally, ethically, and with due regard for the welfare of evaluatees and clients of the evaluations" (11).	• ensure that the superintendent's evaluation adheres to legal and ethical standards • ensure that the work of the superintendent serves the best interests of the schools and students
Utility Standards ...	"are intended to guide evaluations so that they will be informative, timely, and influential" (45).	• provide for an informative and useful superintendent evaluation process • provide evaluation feedback that guides improvement and delivery of high-quality services
Feasibility Standards ...	"call for evaluation systems that are as easy to implement as possible, efficient in their use of time and resources, adequately funded, and viable from a number of other standpoints" (71).	• provide for a practical superintendent evaluation process in light of social, political, and government forces and constraints
Accuracy Standards ...	"require that the obtained information be technically accurate and that conclusions be linked logically to the data" (83).	• offer a basis for determining the soundness of the evaluation in assessing the superintendent's performance

Source: *The Personnel Evaluation Standards*, 1988, pp. 11, 45, 71, & 83.

first letter of the category of standards (e.g., P for propriety). The five Propriety Standards include:

P-1 Service Orientation. Superintendent evaluation should promote sound education and help fulfill the school system's mission so that educational needs of students, community, and society are met.

P-2 Formal Evaluation Guidelines. Guidelines for the superintendent's evaluation should be agreed upon and communicated in appropriate written form (e.g., negotiated contract).

P-3 Conflict of Interest. Conflicts of interest should be identified and properly dealt with to avoid compromising the process and results of the superintendent's evaluation.

P-4 Access to Personnel Evaluation Reports. Conscientiousness should always be followed in providing access to the superintendent's evaluation.

P-5 Interactions with Evaluatees. The superintendent evaluation process should always be conducted in a professional manner in an effort to enhance, and not damage, reputations and performance.

Utility Standards

"Utility Standards are intended to guide evaluations so that they will be informative, timely, and influential" (Joint Committee, 1988, p. 45). As with other educators' evaluations, the evaluation of superintendents should inform decision makers regarding goal accomplishment. While our interests in this book revolve around the superintendent's evaluation, the collective evaluations of all employees should relate individual performance to the overarching organizational goals (Stronge & Helm, 1991). This concept of utility is illuminated in five specific standards:

U-1 Constructive Orientation. The intent and practice of superintendent evaluation should be constructive in order to assist the superintendent in providing excellent service.

U-2 Defined Uses. The intended uses of the evaluation process should be agreed upon in advance in order to facilitate the most appropriate design.

U-3 Evaluator Credibility. The superintendent's evaluation should be conducted credibly and professionally so that the results of the evaluation are respected and used.

U-4 Functional Reporting. Evaluation reports should be clear, timely, accurate, and germane in order to enhance practical value.

U-5 Follow-up and Impact. There should be appropriate follow-up to ensure that the results of the evaluation are understood and that appropriate actions are taken as needed.

Feasibility Standards

The Feasibility Standards state that evaluation systems should be "as easy to implement as possible, efficient in their use of time and resources, adequately funded, and viable from a number of other standpoints" (Joint Committee, 1988, p. 71). An evaluation system that satisfies the Feasibility Standards will be applicable specifically to superintendents while, at the same time, it will be sensitive to the practical issues related to proper evaluation within the school system. The Feasibility category includes three specific standards:

F-1 Practical Procedures. The superintendent's evaluation should be planned and implemented so that the process yields needed information while minimizing disruption and costs.

F-2 Political Viability. A collaborative process should be employed in designing and implementing the superintendent evaluation to make the process more constructive and viable.

F-3 Fiscal Viability. Adequate resources should be provided in order for superintendent evaluation to be implemented effectively and efficiently.

Accuracy Standards

Accuracy Standards state that information must "be technically accurate and that conclusions be linked logically to the data" (Joint Committee, 1988, p. 83). The eight standards within the Accuracy category can be summarized as follows:

A-1 Defined Role. Superintendent evaluation should be based on well-defined job responsibilities.

A-2 Work Environment. The superintendent's performance evaluation is an integrated system in which contextual issues must be considered.

A-3 Documentation of Procedures. The use of multiple data sources should be included in the design of the superintendent's evaluation.

A-4 Valid Measurement. A basic requirement for any quality performance evaluation system is that it be valid for its intended audience.

A-5 Reliable Measurement. In order for valid superintendent evaluation to exist, the system must provide consistent and acceptable performance evaluations procedures.

A-6 Systematic Data Control. Systematic and accurate analysis of data is considered essential for a fair superintendent evaluation system.

A-7 Bias Control. Fairness in both evaluation processes and outcomes can be enhanced by providing proper training to board members who conduct the evaluation.

A-8 Monitoring Evaluation Systems. Periodically monitoring the application of the superintendent evaluation system can help refine and improve the system over time.

HOW IS THE HANDBOOK ORGANIZED?

This chapter addressed the issue of evaluating specialized educational personnel in a manner that will ensure fairness to the individual educator as well as to the school district and community. The focus of all evaluations, including those that have a summative element, should be on improvement. Evaluation is merely a means to an end. Improving individual performance in order to provide quality services and programs to students is the ultimate purpose of evaluation. The intent of this book is to facilitate that effort.

Subsequent chapters in the *Handbook* are organized as outlined in Figure 1.2.

In addition to the chapters, we have included accompanying appendices that contain numerous forms, formats, tools, and techniques intended to make the practical tasks of developing and implementing a

Figure 1.2. Key Steps in Understanding and Designing the Superintendent's Performance Evaluation System

Chapter	Focus
2: Background and History	• What is the history of superintendent evaluation? • What evaluation models can be considered for superintendent evaluation?
3: Performance Standards	• What are the superintendent's major roles and responsibilities upon which the evaluation will be based?
4: Documenting the Superintendent's Performance	• How will performance of the superintendent's job be documented? • How well is the superintendent expected to perform?
5: Implementing the Superintendent's Performance Evaluation	• What is needed in terms of policy, procedures, and training for successful implementation of a superintendent evaluation system?
6: Where Do We Go From Here?	• How do all the pieces fit? • Where do we go from here?

quality superintendent evaluation system easier. Moreover, in developing the *Handbook*, our overarching goal has been to facilitate the design of a fair and comprehensive system for superintendent evaluation that

- connects the superintendent's performance to school board and school district goals and objectives,
- holds superintendents responsible for high but realistic expectations for performance,
- is professionalizing for the superintendent,
- provides opportunities for growth,
- can be objectively assessed using appropriate data sources, and
- is practical to implement.

In the following chapters we attempt to fulfill this goal.

REFERENCES

American Association of School Administrators. (1980). *Evaluating the superintendent.* Arlington, VA: Author.

Candoli, I. C., Cullen, K., & Stufflebeam, D. L. (1997). *Superintendent performance evaluation: Current practice and directions for improvement.* Boston: Kluwer Academic Publishers.

Joint Committee on Standards for Educational Evaluation (D. L. Stufflebeam, Chair). (1988). *The personnel evaluation standards: How to assess systems for evaluating educators.* Newbury Park, CA: Corwin Press, Inc.

MacPhail-Wilcox, B., & Forbes, R. (1990). *Administrator evaluation handbook: How to design a system of administrative evaluation.* Bloomington, IN: Phi Delta Kappa.

Peterson, D. (1989). *Superintendent evaluation.* Eugene, OR: ERIC Clearinghouse on Educational Management. (ERIC Digest Series Number EA 42).

Schaffer, F. M. (1999). *The processes and practices of superintendent performance evaluation in a mid-Atlantic state.* Doctoral dissertation, University of Maryland. (UMI Dissertation Services, UMI No. 9925831).

Stronge, J. H. (In press). Evaluating educational specialists. In D. Nevo & D. Stufflebeam (Eds.), *The international handbook of educational evaluation.* Boston, MA: Kluwer Academic Press.

Stronge, J. H., & Helm, V. J. (1991). *Evaluating professional support personnel.* Newbury Park, CT: Corwin Press.

2

BACKGROUND AND HISTORY

Since the inception of the role of the superintendant, it has evolved in response to changes in the goals of public education and the needs of school boards. Superintendents are the educational experts that guide lay boards of education in the governance of school districts. The nature of the relationships between superintendents and school boards as well as the perceived effectiveness of superintendents also has evolved. In this chapter we provide a historical background and models of evaluation. In particular, we address the following questions

- How has the role of the superintendent changed since its inception?
- What are the critical leadership skills for an effective superintendent?
- What is the history of superintendent evaluation?
- What is the relationship between performance expectations of the superintendent and evaluative criteria used to assess performance?
- What are the purposes of superintendent evaluation?
- What are the merits of different models of superintendent evaluation?

HOW HAS THE ROLE OF THE SUPERINTENDENT CHANGED SINCE ITS INCEPTION?

The first superintendent was appointed in 1837, when the board of education in Buffalo, New York, determined that "a full-time leader was needed to carry out the policies initiated by the board" (cited in Carter & Cunningham, 1997, p. 22). Early generations of superintendents were appointed to solve administrative problems confronting the growth in numbers and in sizes of public schools. Teachers alone were responsible for what happened in classrooms during the nineteenth century and school curricula remained static. By the end of that century, superintendents were common in cities, where they assisted lay school boards in the operation of schools.

The twentieth century emerged with a debate between classicists and modernists concerning curriculum content (Potter, 1967). School populations were growing and virtually all the states had adopted compulsory attendance laws. School boards looked to superintendents to take active roles as the expert educators in the district, guiding curricular decisions and instructional practices. By the mid-1930s, improved roads and motor buses facilitated a trend to consolidate and dramatically reduce the number of one-room schools. The expansion of student enrollment, experiments in curriculum, and legislative enactments affecting curriculum all contributed to a more complex role for school leaders. Consequently, organizational complexity led to a role for superintendents that was primarily "administrative" in nature. Moreover, scientific management practices were adopted from the private sector. Boards became policymaking bodies and school superintendents ran school districts day to day. During ensuing decades, boards wanted expert managers to lead their school districts. Carter and Cunningham called this "the era of the four B's: bonds, buses, budgets, and buildings" (1997, p. 23).

An earned high school diploma, uncommon prior to World War II, became a reality for almost 50 percent of the population by the end of the 1950s. During that decade, a significant event, the launch of Sputnik in 1957, shaped the evolving superintendency. This achievement of the Soviet Union during the Cold War Era changed public expectations of public schools and generated national legislation that dramatically impacted curriculum. Expectations focused on improving schools, and superintendents responded to the challenges. Effective superintendents implemented reforms, advised their boards, interfaced with the public, and became adept political strategists. Yet, definitions of the role of superintendent varied dramatically among school districts.

WHAT ARE THE CRITICAL LEADERSHIP SKILLS FOR AN EFFECTIVE SUPERINTENDENT?

Although the role of the superintendent is broadly defined, there is agreement that the superintendent is the leader of a school district. Warren Bennis (1994) once asserted that more has been written and yet less is known about leadership than any other topic in the social sciences. The designation as "district leader," therefore, adds little clarity to the role. Katz (1955) argued that effective administrators across all disciplines possess basic skill sets. They include

- Technical skills—specialized knowledge, tools, and techniques
- Conceptual skills—ability to see the big picture, and
- Human skills—working with people and ethical dimensions.

In order to explore the multiple and varied dimensions of the role of superintendent, we used this framework of administrative skills to compare the attributes of leaders as described by some of the most notable thinkers and authors on leadership (Figure 2.1).

Note that the representative perspectives of leadership overwhelmingly focus on *Human Skills*—working with people, building relationships, and behaving ethically. The second most important area is *Conceptual Skills*. School district leaders must be able to "see the big picture" in order to provide a vision and plan for the future. These skill areas certainly encompass the broad spectrum of superintendent role definitions and provide insight into the critical skills of effective superintendent leaders.

Figure 2.1. Comparing Leader Attributes

	Technical Skills (special knowledge, tools, and techniques)	Conceptual Skills (ability to see the enterprise as a whole)	Human Skills (working with people, ethical dimensions)
James McGregor Burns (Author of *Government by the People* and *Leadership*)		Considers causative factors (changes in motives and goals)	Draws on the collective strength of individual and group (no leader works in isolation)
			Considers dissenting viewpoints (meaningful conflict)
			Stimulates moral and purposeful growth of followers
			Elevates by transforming principled levels of judgment
John Gardner (Author of *On Leadership, No Easy Victories,* and *Excellence*)	Demonstrates task competence Exhibits capacity to manage	Applies intelligence and judgment to actions and decisions Accepts responsibility willingly Knows followers' needs Harbors need to achieve Exhibits self-confidence	Demonstrates good people skills Motivates others Acts courageously, steadfastly Wins and holds trust Acts assertively in concert with ascendance, dominance Shows ability, flexibility
Stephen Covey (Author of *First Things First, Principle-Centered Leadership,* and *The Seven Habits of Highly Effective People*)	Puts first things first Sharpens the saw	Acts proactively (personal vision) Begins with the end in mind	Thinks win/win Seeks to understand and be understood Utilizes synergy
James Kouzes and Barry Posner (Coauthors of *The Leadership Challenge*)		Challenges the process Inspires a shared vision	Enables others to act Models the way Encourages the heart

Warren Bennis and Burt Nanus (Coauthors of *Leaders: Strategies for Taking Charge*)	Creates meaning & purpose Enrolls people in a vision	Creates social architecture to generate intellectual capital	Generates & sustains trust Has character
Michael Fullan (Author of *Change Forces* and *Leading in a Culture of Change*)	Seeks & makes coherence	Creates & shares knowledge Understands the change process	Has a moral purpose Builds relationships

Adapted from: Stronge, J. H. (1998). Leadership skills in school and business. *The School Administrator*, 55(9), 21–24, 26.

WHAT IS THE HISTORY OF SUPERINTENDENT EVALUATION?

In 1980, an attempt was made to clarify the role of superintendent. Representatives of the American Association of School Administrators (AASA) and National School Boards Association (NSBA) met to define the roles and responsibilities of the superintendent. The joint committee's work generated a publication, *Evaluating the Superintendent* (AASA, 1980), that placed more emphasis on the *process* of conducting an evaluation than the *content* of evaluation. Their meeting also produced a "Joint AASA/NSBA Statement on Superintendent Evaluation" that commented on the prevailing practice of superintendent evaluation and recommended a new process to evaluate superintendents:

> Though individual school board members have many opportunities to observe and evaluate superintendents' performance, it is clear that such informal evaluations cannot provide the board with a complete picture of superintendents' effectiveness in carrying out her (his) complex job. Regular, formal evaluations offer boards the best means of assessing their chief administrator's total performance. Conducted properly they benefit the instructional program of the school district. (AASA, 1980, p. 4)

However, the attention paid to systemically developing and implementing a performance-based evaluation system for superintendents since that time has been uneven at best.

Another event that had a dramatic impact on the role of superintendents was the publication in 1983 of *A Nation at Risk*. This report from

the National Commission on Excellence in Education (1983) categorized America's public schools as mediocre and contended that they had
placed the future of the nation in jeopardy. The report's major recommendations included

- establishing a core curriculum,
- raising academic standards,
- increasing instructional time,
- improving teacher quality, and
- recruiting and employing more capable teachers.

The report spawned a plethora of other studies and reports that focused
on how to improve American public schools. Politicians were quick to
jump on the bandwagon and legislate "fixes" for the public schools. The
resulting wave of national and state reforms, including the establishment
of standards and accountability measures, placed the public's eye on the
quality issue once more. This time, however, the focus was on improving
student achievement. The resulting impact on the expectations and roles
of all school professionals, including superintendents, was dramatic.

In an attempt to define the profession of the superintendency, AASA
established a commission (1992) that developed a set of eight professional standards and a corresponding set of competencies (Figure 2.2).
It was an attempt to stabilize a profession that was confronted by multiple constituencies with different, and often competing, expectations,
priorities, and agendas.

The AASA and NSBA convened a joint committee again in 1994 to
review the changing environment and resulting modifications in roles
and relationships. They identified various "Superintendent Responsibilities" that we categorized under their corresponding AASA Professional
Standards (Figure 2.3). Note that the 1992 committee focused on personal competencies required to meet the standards (see Figure 2.2)
while the 1994 committee targeted the professional responsibilities superintendents have under each standard (see Figure 2.3).

It is interesting to note that as recently as 1994, when the joint committee defined the eighteen superintendent responsibilities, the responsibilities reflected neither *Curriculum Planning and Development*
nor *Instructional Management*, two of the eight professional standards
directly addressing instructional leadership. The potential impact of

Leadership and District Culture
- Demonstrate an awareness of international issues affecting schools and students.
- Maintain personal, physical, and emotional wellness.
- Promote and model risk taking.
- Facilitate comparative planning between constituencies.
- Promote the value of understanding and celebrating school/community cultures.

Policy and Governance
- Describe the system of public school governance in our democracy.
- Relate local policy to state and federal regulations and requirements.
- Describe procedures to avoid civil and criminal liabilities.

Communications and Community Relations
- Demonstrate an understanding of political theory and skills needed to build community support for district priorities.
- Demonstrate that good judgment and actions communicate as well as words.
- Develop formal and informal techniques to gain external perceptions of district by means of surveys, advisory groups, and personal contact.
- Communicate and project an articulate position for education.
- Write clearly and forcefully.
- Demonstrate formal and informal listening skills.
- Identify political forces in a community.
- Identify the political context of the community environment.
- Formulate strategies for passing referenda.
- Identify, track, and deal with issues.

Organizational Management
- Define the major components of quality management.
- Discuss legal concepts, regulations, and codes for school operations.
- Describe the process of delegating responsibility for decision making.
- Use technological applications to enhance administration of business and support systems.
- Demonstrate planning and scheduling of personal time and organization.

Curriculum Planning and Development
- Develop core curriculum design and delivery systems for diverse school communities.
- Describe curriculum planning/future methods to anticipate occupational trends and their educational implications for lifelong learners.
- Demonstrate an understanding of instructional taxonomies, goal objectives, and processes.
- Describe cognitive development and learning theories and their importance to the sequencing of instruction.
- Demonstrate an understanding of child and adolescent growth and development.
- Describe a process to create developmentally appropriate curriculum and instructional practices for all children and adolescents.
- Demonstrate the use of computers and other technologies in educational programming.
- Conduct assessments of present and future student learning needs.
- Develop a process for faculty input in continued and systematic renewal to ensure appropriate scope, sequence, and content.

continued

Figure 2.2.   AASA Professional Standards and Related Competencies

- Demonstrate an understanding of curricular alignment to ensure improved student performance and higher order thinking.

Instructional Management
- Demonstrate an understanding of motivation in the instructional process.
- Describe classroom management theories and techniques.
- Demonstrate an understanding of the development of the whole student including the physical, social, emotional, cognitive, and linguistic needs.
- Describe instructional strategies that include multicultural sensitivity and diverse learning styles.
- Exhibit applications of computer technology connected to instruction programs.
- Describe how to interpret and use testing/assessment results to improve education.
- Demonstrate knowledge of research findings on the use of a variety of instructional strategies.

Human Resources Management
- Demonstrate knowledge of adult learning theory and motivation.
- Diagnose and improve organizational health and morale.
- Demonstrate personnel management strategies.
- Understand alternative benefit packages.
- Assess individual and institutional sources of stress and develop methods for reducing stress (e.g. counseling, exercise programs, and diet).
- Demonstrate knowledge of pupil personnel service and categorical programs.

Values and Ethics of Leadership
- Describe the role of schooling in a democratic society.
- Describe a strategy to promote the value that moral and ethical practices are established and practiced in each classroom and school.
- Describe a strategy to ensure that diversity of religion, ethnicity, and way of life in the district are respected.
- Formulate a plan to coordinate social, health, and community agencies to support each child in the district.

Figure 2.2. *continued*

high-stakes testing had not yet substantially affected the performance evaluations of superintendents.

This lack of focus on instruction and increased academic performance was evidenced by the criteria commonly used by school boards to evaluate superintendent performance as reported by Glass (1992). The top five, in rank order, were

- general effectiveness,
- board/superintendent relations,
- management functions,
- budget development and implementation, and
- educational leadership/knowledge.

Leadership and District Culture
- To serve as the school board's chief executive officer and preeminent educational adviser in all efforts of the board to fulfill its school system governance role.
- To propose and institute a process for long-range strategic planning that will engage the board and the community in positioning the school district for success in ensuing years.
- To develop a description for the board of what constitutes leadership and management of public schools, taking into account that effective leadership and management are the results of effective governance and effective administration combined.
- To collaborate with other administrators through national and state professional associations to inform state legislators, members of Congress, and all other appropriate state and federal officials of local concerns and issues.

Policy and Governance
- To serve as a catalyst for the school system's administrative leadership team in proposing and implementing policy changes.
- To present policy options along with specific recommendations to the board when circumstances require the board to adopt new policies or review existing policies.
- To develop and inform the board of administrative procedures needed to implement board policy.

Communications and Community Relations
- To keep all board members informed about school operations and programs.
- To interpret the needs of the school system to the board.
- To develop a sound program of school/community relations in concert with the board.
- To develop and carry out a plan for keeping the professional and support staff informed about the mission, goals, and strategies of the school system and about important roles all staff members play in realizing them.
- To provide all board members with complete background information and a recommendation for school board action on each agenda item well in advance of each board meeting.
- To develop and implement a continuing plan for working with the news media.

Organizational Management
- To serve as the primary educational leader for the school system and chief administrative officer of the entire school district's professional and support staff, including staff members assigned to provide support service to the board.
- To oversee management of the district's day-to-day operations.

Curriculum Planning and Development
- None

Instructional Management
- None

Human Resources Management
- To ensure that professional development opportunities are available to all school system employees.
- To evaluate personnel performance in harmony with district policy and to keep the board informed about such evaluations.

Values and Ethics of Leadership
- To ensure that the school system provides equal opportunity for all students.

Figure 2.3.   AASA Professional Standards and Superintendent Responsibilities

Expectations and Performance Assessment: The Disconnect

Comprehensive studies of the superintendency in the 1990s (Glass, 1992; Robinson & Bickers, 1990; Stufflebeam, 1994) revealed some disturbing patterns in the process of superintendent evaluation. Although about 90 percent of superintendents nationally were evaluated annually, less than 10 percent of the superintendents said that their board discussed explicit guidelines and performance standards with them when they were hired. The various researchers also found that superintendents were not really evaluated against criteria in their job descriptions. Additionally, these studies confirmed that evaluations leading to termination were too often grounded in personality and board relationship issues. Hoyle and Skrla (1999) contended that a superintendent may receive the highest ratings on most of the evaluation criteria but be nonrenewed due to personality conflicts and politics that are beyond the superintendent's control. Two evaluative criteria stood out in these studies as most important in practice: board/superintendent relationships and general effectiveness of performance.

Even more telling were the two criteria identified as having "little or no" importance in evaluative process: student achievement outcomes and student/superintendent relationships.

By the middle of the 1990s high-stakes tests were established in virtually all states. The constant comparison of schools and school districts by their students' scores on state tests put school system leaders in the "fish bowl" of accountability. The expectations and role of the superintendent quickly evolved in the direction of improving student achievement. Local boards and board members across the nation "heard" the public concern and by 2000, the NSBA proclaimed that the "key work" of school boards was improving student achievement (Gemberling, Smith, & Villani, 2000, p. 1).

As we begin the new century, effective superintendents must possess political and managerial expertise to successfully lead school districts (Johnson, 1996). They, more than ever, also must be instructional leaders, whose responsibilities reach into the heart of classrooms—student learning. This new role is reflected at the beginning of this twenty-first century by the top four expectations school boards have of superintendents. They are, in rank order

- educational leader,
- political leader,

- managerial leader, and
- leader of reform. (Glass, Bjork, & Brunner, 2000)

A comparison of evaluation criteria most commonly used up to the early 1990s with these expectations, in rank order, reveal the changing expectations of the performance of superintendents that boards use to evaluate their performance (Figure 2.4).

Figure 2.4. Comparison of Evaluation Criteria 1992 and Board Expectations 2000

1992	2000
General effectiveness	Educational leader
Board/superintendent relations	Political leader
Management functions	Managerial leader
Budget development and implementation	Leader of reform

Sources: Glass, 1992; Glass, Bjork & Bruner, 2000.

Evaluations should be based in the generic duties of particular professional groups (Scriven, 1994). Determining job expectations is a logical and necessary initial step in designing a superintendent evaluation system. Doing so bases performance assessment on the professional competencies and duties of the position (Candoli, Cullen, & Stufflebeam, 1997; Stronge, 1997). Superintendents are the chief executive officers of school districts: "Executives, by definition, are considered to be responsible for organizational outcomes whether or not they exercise direct influence over the achievement of outcomes" (Duke, 1992, p. 114). Although there is increasing consensus that assessments of student progress must be used in educational evaluation (Candoli, et al., 1997), student learning alone does not capture the realm of public expectations nor does it capture the day-to-day realities of the responsibilities of school superintendents.

WHAT ARE THE PURPOSES OF SUPERINTENDENT EVALUATION?

Superintendents often quip that board members are only willing to devote the time required to perform a formal evaluation when they are not satisfied with their superintendent's performance and are attempting to terminate their superintendent's employment. Superintendents are the only school system employees not supervised or evaluated by another licensed professional. Yet, superintendents must be evaluated. Most states have adopted legislation requiring boards to regularly evaluate their superintendents. Besides fulfilling a legal requirement, the process can be a valuable tool and serve a broad range of purposes, such as

- defining the board's expectations of the superintendent,
- enhancing superintendent/board communications,
- identifying and prioritizing school system goals,
- clarifying the roles of the board and superintendent,
- improving board/superintendent relations,
- enhancing the planning process,
- improving educational performance,
- making personnel decisions, and
- holding the superintendent accountable.

Superintendents want and need feedback from their boards. It is difficult to grow professionally without it. Evaluations provide superintendents an opportunity to assess their board's satisfaction with their performance. The evaluation process also gives board members an opportunity to assess the superintendent's job satisfaction.

Models of Performance Assessment

In an effort to improve the evaluation of superintendents in America's school systems, the Center for Research on Educational Accountability and Teacher Evaluation (CREATE) completed a research project to provide "the foundation for future development of improved models for evaluating school district superintendents" (Candoli et al., 1997, p. 7). They described and assessed current evaluation models and provided a draft of an "improved" model that attempts to consider multifaceted superintendent performance in evaluating overall performance.

The study by CREATE identified twelve distinct models of superintendent evaluation. In their report, the models were categorized by the three general methods used to draw conclusions from the evaluation process: (1) global judgment, (2) judgment driven by criteria, and (3) judgment driven by data.

- *Global Judgment* consisted of several prominent evaluation practices, including school board judgment, descriptive narrative reports, and/or formative exchanges about performance.
- *Judgment Driven by Criteria* may have consisted of printed rating forms, report cards, management by objectives (MBO), performance contracting, and/or duties-based evaluation. This category is comparable to results-focused appraisals of business models.
- *Judgment Driven by Data* was also related to the results-focused appraisals of business models and includes superintendent portfolios, student outcome measures, and school and district accreditation.

Figure 2.5 depicts the twelve models as they were categorized.

CREATE researchers evaluated each of the identified models using the personnel evaluation standards established by the Joint Committee on Standards for Educational Evaluation (1988). All of the models evaluated contained relative strengths and weaknesses. However, those that have the greatest potential to meet the essential criteria for quality personnel evaluation (Candoli et al., 1997; Joint Committee on Standards for Educational Evaluation, 1988) include

- duties-based evaluation,
- superintendent portfolios, and
- the use of student outcome measures.

Figure 2.5. Superintendent Evaluation Models

Global Judgment	Judgment Driven by Specified Criteria	Judgment Driven by Data
Board Judgment	Printed Rating Forms	Superintendent Portfolio
Descriptive Narrative Reports	Report Cards	Student Outcome Measures
Formative Exchanges About	Management by Objectives	School and District
Performance	Performance Contracting	Accreditation
Stakeholder Evaluation	Duties-Based Evaluation	

Adapted from: DiPaola, M. F., & Stronge, J. H. (2001). Superintendent evaluation in a standards-based environment: A status report from the states. *Journal of Personnel Evaluation in Education, 15*(2), 97–110.

Including these features in superintendent evaluation would enable boards to enjoy the benefits of the strengths of each model while compensating for individual models' weaknesses.

Board members are most often lay people with a primary orientation to and knowledge of assessment models used in the private sector. A comparison of the Candoli, Cullen, and Stufflebeam superintendent evaluation models with business evaluation models (Grote, 1996) reveals considerable overlap between the two worlds, as presented in Figure 2.6.

The comparison of the models from the two sectors indicated

- *Global Judgment* is closely related to the global appraisals proposed by Grote (1996) in describing business models. They represent the simplest of appraisals and rely on the raters' knowledge of the overall performance of the superintendent and require well-trained appraisers.
- *Judgment Driven by Criteria* corresponds and overlaps with both results-focused and behaviorally anchored business models. Rating

Figure 2.6.   Comparison of Business Appraisal and Superintendent Evaluation Models

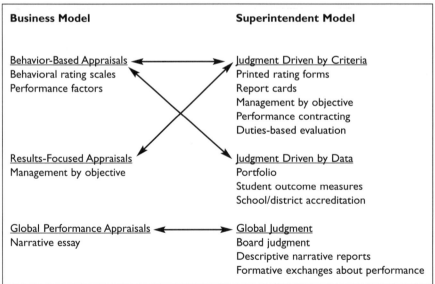

Adapted from: DiPaola, M. F., & Stronge, J. H. (2001). Superintendent evaluation in a standards-based environment: A status report from the states. *Journal of Personnel Evaluation in Education, 15*(2), 97–110.

scales, specified performance factors, outcome measures, and objectives drive these appraisals.

- *Judgment Driven by Data* is closely related to the behaviorally anchored business model. This model is duties-based with a focus on performance and outcome measures.

This comparison may help board members see the similarities to assessment models with which they have more familiarity.

Evaluation of Superintendents across the Nation

In 2000, we completed a national study of the fifty states to assess current policies and practices in superintendent evaluation. In our efforts to find what each state required or recommended in evaluating school superintendents, representatives of all state education agencies and each state affiliate of the NSBA and AASA were telephoned to ascertain whether guidelines or policies in superintendent evaluation were offered or required. They also were queried concerning their distribution of preferred/recommended models of superintendent evaluation.

The professional affiliates in eight states (California, Delaware, Florida, Indiana, Iowa, Kansas, Maine, and Nevada) reported neither having state guidelines nor providing recommended guidelines or instruments to their constituents. We collected state guidelines and/or procedures (where they existed) as well as recommended evaluation instruments and related materials from the other forty-two states. Materials collected and analyzed as part of our national study included (1) a description of evaluation guidelines and/or processes, (2) copies of paradigm evaluation instruments, and (3) copies of state-mandated evaluation procedures (where available).

We performed a content analysis on all collected materials (Berg, 2001). The analysis compared recommended superintendent evaluation models to the *AASA Professional Standards for the Superintendency* to determine to what extent the performance criteria in current practice were compatible with the professional standards. We made frequency counts of full and partial matches to the AASA Professional Standards. Although the AASA Professional Standards were reflected in materials gathered from forty-two states, the manner in which they were articulated varied greatly from state to state. We found that only the recommended evaluation materials from Hawaii, Oregon, and Texas fully matched all of the AASA Professional Standards. Organizational management was the most common standard reflected in state evaluation information (88 percent). The least common standard reflected was values and ethics of leadership (26 percent). Figure 2.7 provides frequency counts of the standards contained in this national study.

We also categorized the state models using the twelve Models of Superintendent Performance Evaluation (Candoli et al., 1997) to assess the general orientations of evaluation practices and determine which models were most frequently employed. Frequency counts were made of full and partial matches to the twelve Models of Superintendent Performance Evaluation. Figure 2.8 provides a summary of superintendent evaluation models as recommended by the respective state departments of education, the state AASA affiliates, and/or the state NSBA affiliates. Please note that where more than one model is indicated for a state, more than one evaluation system was recommended by the state education agency or NSBA/AASA affiliate.

WHAT ARE THE MERITS OF DIFFERENT MODELS OF SUPERINTENDENT EVALUATION?

We used the most prominent features reflected in the superintendent evaluation systems to categorize the systems per the various models. Two

Figure 2.7. Frequency of AASA Professional Standards for the Superintendency (as noted in state-recommended evaluation models)

	Match		
	Full	*Partial*	*No*
Leadership and District Culture	4	27	11
Policy and Governance	3	30	9
Communications and Community Relations	3	32	7
Organizational Management	3	34	5
Curriculum Planning and Development	3	22	17
Instructional Management	3	23	16
Human Resources Management	3	32	7
Values and Ethics of Leadership	3	8	31

Figure 2.8. Superintendent Performance Evaluation Models (as noted in state-recommended evaluation models)

State*	Global Judgment				Judgment Driven by Specified Criteria				Judgment Driven by Data			
	Board Judgment	Descriptive Narrative Reports	Formative Exchanges about Performance	Stakeholder Evaluation	Printed Rating Forms	Report Cards	Management by Objectives	Performance Contracting	Duties-Based Evaluation	Superintendent Portfolio	Student Outcome Measures	School and District Accreditation
AL	✓	°	°	°	✓	°	°	°	✓	°	✓	°
AK	°	°	°	°	✓	°	°	°	°	°	°	°
AZ	°	°	°	✓	✓	°	✓	°	°	°	°	°
AR	°	°	°	°	✓	°	✓	°	°	°	°	°
CA												
CO	°	°	°	°	✓	°	°	°	✓	°	°	°
CT	°	°	°	°	✓	°	✓	°	°	°	°	°
DE												
FL												
GA	°	°	°	°	✓	°	°	°	✓	°	°	°
HI	✓	°	°	°	✓	°	✓	°	°	°	°	°
ID	✓	°	°	°	°	°	°	°	°	°	°	°
IL	°	°	°	°	✓	°	✓	°	°	°	°	°
IO												
IA												
KS												
KY	°	°	°	°	✓	°	✓	✓	✓	°	✓	°
LA	°	°	°	°	✓	°	✓	✓	✓	°	°	°
MA	°	°	°	°	✓	°	✓	°	°	°	°	°
ME												
MD	✓	°	°	°	°	°	°	°	°	°	°	°
MI	°	°	°	°	✓	°	°	°	°	°	°	°
MN	°	°	°	°	✓	°	✓	°	°	°	°	°
MS	✓	°	°	°	✓	°	°	°	°	°	°	°
MO	°	°	✓	°	✓	°	✓	°	°	°	°	°
MT	°	✓	°	°	✓	°	°	°	°	°	°	°
NE	°	°	✓	°	✓	°	✓	°	°	°	°	°
NV												
NH	°	°	°	°	°	°	✓	°	°	°	°	°
NJ	°	°	°	°	✓	°	✓	°	°	°	°	°
NM	°	°	°	°	°	°	°	°	°	°	°	°
NY	✓	✓	°	✓	°	✓	°	°	°	°	°	°
NC	°	°	°	°	✓	°	✓	°	°	°	°	°
ND	°	°	✓	°	✓	°	°	°	°	°	°	°
OH	°	°	°	°	✓	°	✓	°	°	°	°	°
OK	°	°	°	°	✓	°	✓	°	°	°	°	°

Figure 2.8. continued

State*	Global Judgment				Judgment Driven by Specified Criteria				Judgment Driven by Data			
	Board Judgment	Descriptive Narrative Reports	Formative Exchanges about Performance	Stakeholder Evaluation	Printed Rating Forms	Report Cards	Management by Objectives	Performance Contracting	Duties-Based Evaluation	Superintendent Portfolio	Student Outcome Measures	School and District Accreditation
OR	°	°	✓	°	✓	°	✓	°	°	°	°	°
PA	°	°	°	°	✓	°	✓	°	°	°	°	°
RI	°	°	°	°	✓	°	°	°	°	°	°	°
SC	°	°	°	°	✓	°	✓	°	°	°	°	°
SD	°	°	°	°	✓	°	°	°	°	°	°	°
TN	°	°	°	°	✓	°	✓	✓	°	°	✓	°
TX	°	°	✓	°	✓	°	✓	°	✓	✓	✓	°
UT	°	°	°	°	°	°	✓	✓	°	°	°	°
VT	°	✓	✓	✓	✓	°	✓	°	°	°	✓	✓
VA	°	°	°	°	✓	°	✓	°	°	°	°	°
WA	°	°	°	°	°	°	°	°	✓	°	°	°
WV	✓	°	°	°	°	°	°	°	°	°	°	°
WI	°	°	✓	°	✓	°	✓	°	°	°	°	°
WY	°	°	°	°	✓	✓	°	°	°	°	°	°

* Provided by state school board association and/or AASA affiliate
✓ = Fully or partially present
▨ = No report
° = Indicator absent

or more superintendent evaluation models were recommended by 32 percent of the states that responded. The remaining 68 percent provided evaluation information that was representative of only one of the models. Management by objectives and printed rating forms were the most commonly used forms of evaluation, with 89 percent of states using some variation of printed rating forms and 68 percent of the states embedding MBO into their performance evaluations. Candoli, Cullen, and Stufflebeam (1997) enumerated eighteen strengths and twenty-six weaknesses for printed rating forms. Strengths included factors such as clarification of expectations, comprehensiveness, characteristics of open-endedness and structure, inclusion of multiple perspectives, and ease of use. Weaknesses included factors such as having little stakeholder involvement, being out-of-date or having inadequate job requirements, being too general, lacking congruence to the responsibilities of the superintendency, and lacking provisions for professional development.

Candoli, Cullen, and Stufflebeam (1997) also identified thirteen areas of strength and nine areas of weakness in MBO. The strengths included: forced recognition of current priority for objectives, clear authority given to the board for evaluation, flexibility, encouragement of dialogue between the board and the superintendent, and ease in implementation. Weaknesses included watering down of objectives, neglect of student learning concerns, having no provisions for stakeholders, and objectives not reflecting actual job performance.

All of the models in this analysis contain relative strengths and weaknesses. However, *evaluation models in which strengths overshadowed weaknesses include duties-based evaluation and superintendent portfolio.* In our study, only one of the responding states employed superintendent portfolios and seven (16.6 percent) used duties-based evaluations.

We found that of the evaluation processes in use, the vast majority have their roots in scientific management (Hoyle & Skrla, 1999). As noted earlier, the data revealed that printed rating forms (checklists) and MBO are the predominant evaluation models used in the superintendent evaluation process. These models in isolation neither adequately give superintendents a chance to really understand the board's satisfaction with their performance nor provide the board with an assessment of the superintendent's job satisfaction.

Chapter 1 provides an overview of the application of Personnel Evaluation Standards to superintendents. Evaluation materials we analyzed did not meet all of the essential standards for quality personnel evaluation. These essential standards include

- propriety standards related to legal and ethical considerations;
- utility standards related to the timely, informative, and influential nature of the evaluation;
- feasibility standards related to ease of implementation; and
- accuracy standards related to technical accuracy of information obtained. (Joint Committee on Personnel Evaluation Standards, 1988)

The essential criterion most absent in this study was the accuracy standard. The accuracy standard requires valid, reliable, and systematic data, free from bias. Since school board members are not always trained adequately to complete evaluations to meet this standard, the fairness of evaluations becomes a critical issue.

SUMMARY

The hue and cry for accountability at all levels demands the fair evaluation of all personnel, including the superintendent. We suggest that a fair evaluation of the superintendent requires greater congruence among

- district goals,
- evaluation instruments,
- actual duties performed by superintendents, and
- standards that guide the profession.

At the same time, the evaluation models and evidence of achievement must be well suited to meet all the standards for quality personnel evaluation.

REFERENCES

American Association of School Administrators. (1980). *Evaluating the superintendent.* Arlington, VA: Author.

American Association of School Administrators. (1993). *Professional standards for the superintendency.* Arlington, VA: Author.

Bennis, W. (1994). *On becoming a leader.* Reading, MA: Addison-Wesley Publishing Company.

Berg, B. L. (2001). *Qualitative research methods for the social sciences* (4th ed.). Boston: Allyn and Bacon.

Candoli, I. C., Cullen, K., & Stufflebeam, D. L. (1997). *Superintendent performance evaluation: Current practice and directions for improvement.* Boston: Kluwer Academic Publishers.

Carter, G. R., & Cunningham, W. G. (1997). *The American school superintendent: Leading in an age of pressure.* San Francisco: Jossey-Bass.

DiPaola, M. F., & Stronge, J. H. (2001). Superintendent evaluation in a standards-based environment: A status report from the states. *Journal of Personnel Evaluation in Education, 15*(2), 97–110.

Duke, D. (1992). Concepts of administrative effectiveness and the evaluation of school administrators. *Journal of Personnel Evaluation in Education, 6*(2), 103–122.

Gemberling, K. W., Smith, C. W., & Villani, J. S. (2000). *The keywork of school boards guidebook.* Alexandria, VA: National School Board Association.

Glass, T. E. (1992). *The 1992 study of the American superintendency.* Arlington, VA: American Association of School Administrators.

Glass, T. E., Bjork, L., & Brunner, C. C. (2000). *The study of the American school superintendency: A look at the superintendent of education in the new millennium.* Arlington, VA: American Association of School Administrators.

Grote, D. (1996). Th*e complete guide to performance appraisal.* New York: American Management Association.

Hoyle, J. R., & Skrla, L. (1999). The politics of superintendent evaluation. *Journal of Personnel Evaluation in Education, 13*(4), 405–419.

Johnson, S. M. (1996). *Leading to change: The challenge of the new superintendency.* San Francisco: Jossey-Bass.

Joint Committee on Standards for Educational Evaluation (D. L. Stufflebeam, Chair). (1988). *The personnel evaluation standards: How to assess systems for evaluating educators.* Newbury Park, CA: Corwin Press, Inc.

Joint Committee on Standards for Educational Evaluation. (1994). *The program evaluation standards.* Newbury, VA: Sage.

Katz, R. L. (1955). Skills of an effective administrator. *Harvard Business Review, 33*(1), 33–42.

National Commission on Excellence in Education. (1983). *A nation at risk: The imperative for educational reform.* Washington, DC: U.S. Government Printing Office.

Potter, R. E. (1967). *The stream of American education.* New York: American Book Company.

Robinson, G., & Bickers, P. (1990). *Evaluation of superintendents and school boards.* Arlington, VA: Educational Research Service.

Scriven, M. (1994). Duties of the teacher. *Journal of Personnel Evaluation in Education, 8*(2), 151–184.

Stronge, J. H. (Ed.). (1997). *Evaluating teaching: A guide to current thinking and best practice.* Thousand Oaks, CA: Corwin Press.

Stufflebeam, D. L. (1994). Evaluation of superintendent performance toward a general model. In A. McConney (Ed.), *Toward a unified model: The foundations of personnel evaluation* (pp. 35–90). Kalamazoo, MI: Center for Research on Educational Accountability and Teacher Evaluation [CREATE].

❸

PERFORMANCE STANDARDS: THE FOUNDATION FOR SUPERINTENDENT EVALUATION

The foundation of an effective performance evaluation system in education, including for superintendents, is the use of clearly described and well-documented performance standards. In order for an evaluation to be fair and comprehensive, it is necessary to describe the standards for superintendents with sufficient detail and accuracy so that both the superintendent and those evaluating her or him can reasonably understand the expectations of the job. In essence, what performance standards do is guarantee that the superintendent is evaluated based on what she or he was hired to do! And, in so doing, the job standards serve as the cornerstone of the performance evaluation system.

In this chapter, we explore the processes and products related to the design of the superintendent's performance standards. In particular, we address the following questions

1. What are performance standards?
2. How can superintendent performance standards be used in building an evaluation system in a specific school district setting?
3. What is the relationship between the superintendent performance standards and other standards?
4. What is the relationship between the superintendent performance standards and the superintendent's job description?

WHAT ARE PERFORMANCE STANDARDS?

While various approaches could be employed to describe the job of the superintendent, we have chosen to base the evaluation system upon a three-tiered description of performance as depicted in Figure 3.1.

Domains

Domains reflect the framework for describing major aspects of the work of educators. Basically, domains are categories of job expectations and serve as logical clusters for those job expectations. In other words, domains are categories or placeholders for the superintendent's specific performance standards. The domains provide the framework for describing the major aspects of the job.

We have included a model for consideration in designing domains for superintendents. As presented in Figure 3.2, this role description is based on a combination of a sociopolitical and a functional perspective of the superintendent's role.

Performance Standards

Performance standards are the job responsibilities or duties performed by an educator. They provide greater specification of role ex-

Figure 3.1.   Three-tiered system for performance standards. Figure used with permission of James H. Stronge.

Figure 3.2. Descriptions of Superintendent Performance Domains

Domain	Description
Policy and Governance	This domain describes the job standards related to the policy, governance, and political dimensions of the position.
Planning and Assessment	This domain includes job standards for assessing instructional programs and personnel and for developing improvement plans to promote student learning.
Instructional Leadership	This domain relates to providing vision, direction, motivation, and support to achieve the school district's stated mission and goals. Additionally, this domain focuses on the support and leadership provided in the areas of personnel, curriculum, and staff development for the explicit purpose of enhancing instructional programs.
Organizational Management	This domain relates to supporting, managing, and directing the operations and functions of the organization.
Communications and Community Relations	This domain includes the standards for demonstrating effective communication that promotes understanding, support, and continuous improvement of the school district's programs and services.
Professionalism	This domain includes the standards for demonstrating a commitment to professional ethics and growth while advancing the mission of the organization.

pectations but are broader in nature than discrete, observable behaviors. Performance standards are the duties performed by a superintendent. They are organized into the six general domains identified earlier. They also are intended to provide greater clarity on the precise nature of the domain but do not provide a specific behavior or set of behaviors that would be directly amenable to assessment. An example of a superintendent performance standard within the domain of Instructional Leadership is listed below (Figure 3.3).

Superintendent Performance Standard L-1

The superintendent communicates a clear vision of excellence and continuous improvement consistent with the goals of the school district.

Figure 3.3. Sample performance standard L-1

A complete set of superintendent performance standards, organized by the six previously identified domains, is provided in Appendix A.

Performance Indicators

Performance indicators are used in the superintendent's evaluation system to do just what the term implies—*indicate* in observable behaviors the types and quality of performance associated with the major job responsibilities (performance standards). Performance indicators constitute the most specific description of performance standards in the three-tiered hierarchy and lend themselves nicely to documentation and direct assessment. Typically, there will be two to six performance indicators used to define each performance standard. However, it is important to note that performance indicators are typically *not* used as the unit of evaluation; rather, they are provided to highlight what a superintendent would do if she or he were properly fulfilling the job requirement. Examples of performance indicators for the superintendent Instructional Leadership standard L-1 (Figure 3.3) are listed in Figure 3.4.

The superintendent . . .

- demonstrates personal commitment to achieving the mission of the school district.
- articulates a shared vision to all constituencies and ensures that staff members are working in concert with the district's strategic plan.
- informs members of the board and community of current research related to best practices in curriculum and instruction.
- explores, disseminates, and applies knowledge and information about new or improved methods of instruction or related issues.
- shares evaluation data and subsequent plans for continuous improvement with staff, students, and other stakeholders.
- recognizes, encourages, and celebrates excellence among staff and students.
- demonstrates strong motivation and high standards and models self-evaluation.
- fosters positive morale and team spirit.

Figure 3.4.   Sample Performance Indicators for Standard L-I

Performance indicators such as these have been developed for each performance standard. The sample performance indicators are not intended to be all inclusive lists but rather examples of typical behaviors that indicate satisfactory performance of the applicable standard by a superintendent.

In summary, performance indicators

- are the observable activities that relate to the performance of the job responsibilities,

- are representative of a particular job responsibility,
- can be objectively documented and measured, and
- are intended merely as samples and not as a full set of behaviors for any job.

A set of suggested superintendent performance indicators, along with domains and performance standards, is located in Appendix A.

HOW CAN SUPERINTENDENT PERFORMANCE STANDARDS BE USED IN BUILDING AN EVALUATION IN A SPECIFIC SCHOOL DISTRICT SETTING?

Domains, the first tier used in defining the job of superintendents, identify major categories of work, and *performance indicators*, the third tier, serve as examples of behaviors that will be observed or documented. However, it is the *performance standards* that are the basic building blocks of the evaluation system. In most performance evaluation systems, the performance standards are viewed as the explicit job requirements for the superintendent and all applicable standards must be fulfilled in order to meet job expectations. Remember, for summative evaluation ratings, superintendents typically are evaluated on each standard. In some instances, school boards prefer to give an aggregate—or overall—rating for the major domains. However, the performance indicators definitely should not be used for summative ratings as they are intended merely to serve as suggested activities and behaviors that shed light on the performance standards.

The list of superintendent performance standards included in this book are intended to be as comprehensive as possible. However, we do *not* intend that an entire list be implemented verbatim because—

- In order for one person to implement all of the duties identified for a position in any meaningful fashion, it would require the proverbial 110 percent effort. In most cases it just isn't practical to attempt to do everything.
- Even if it *is* feasible to implement all of the identified performance standards, it probably isn't desirable. Expectations and needs vary

from one organization to another, and even within the same school district there frequently is the need to refocus or redefine the job from time to time. This factor needs to be considered in designing the superintendent's job and selecting the specific performance standards to be emphasized.

- The context of the job needs to be considered when defining it. For example, some of the performance standards listed for the super-intendent may be more appropriate in some school districts than in others. The performance standards included in the performance evaluation should reflect these differences in assignment from school district to school district.

WHAT IS THE RELATIONSHIP BETWEEN THE SUPERINTENDENT PERFORMANCE EVALUATION STANDARDS AND OTHER GUIDELINES?

In designing and field-testing the six domains and related job standards for superintendents, we gave careful attention to how well they fit with existing professional guidelines and standards related to superintendent work. In particular, we were attentive to

- the American Association for School Administrators' (AASA) pro-fessional standards for the superintendency (1993),
- the roles of the superintendent as identified by the National School Board Association (Gemberling, Smith, & Villani, 2000),
- the Interstate School Leaders Licensure Consortium Standards (ISLLC) (Council of Chief State School Officers [CCSSO], 1996), and
- Technology Standards for School Administrators (TSSA Collaborative, 2001).

American Association of School Administrators Recommended Standards

In an effort to define the profession of the superintendency, AASA established a commission that developed a set of eight professional standards and a corresponding set of competencies (AASA, 1993). The

Commission stated that "all superintendents should be held accountable for the eight professional standards" (Carter & Cunningham, 1997, p. 17). Further, in 1998, AASA published skills/standards for successful twenty-first-century school leaders (Hoyle, English, & Steffy, 1998). The AASA standards consist of the eight interrelated standards as depicted in Figure 3.5.

Figure 3.5. American Association of School Administrators Superintendent Standards

AASA Standard	Key Descriptors
Standard 1: Leadership and District Culture	Vision, academic rigor, excellence, empowerment, problem solving
Standard 2: Policy and Governance	Policy formulation, democratic processes, regulations
Standard 3: Communications and Community Relations	Internal and external communications, community support, consensus building
Standard 4: Organizational Management	Data-driven decision making, problem solving, operations management and reporting
Standard 5: Curriculum Planning and Development	Curriculum planning, instructional design, human growth and development
Standard 6: Instructional Management	Student achievement, classroom management, instructional technology
Standard 7: Human Resources Management	Personnel induction, development, evaluation, compensation, organizational health
Standard 8: Values and Ethics of Leadership	Multicultural and ethnic understanding, personal integrity and ethics

Note: The AASA superintendency standards are described in more detail in chapter 2.

National School Boards Association Recommended Standards

In 2000, the National School Boards Association (NSBA) published a guide to assist local school boards in focusing efforts on their key work—increasing student achievement (Gemberling et al., 2000). The authors of the NSBA book argue that this systemic approach results in high-quality schools with student achievement as their primary focus. The guide defines the roles of both the board and superintendent in each of eight "key action areas" that include

- vision,
- standards,
- assessment,
- accountability,
- alignment,
- climate,
- collaboration, and
- continuous improvement. (Gemberling et al., 2000)

Interstate School Leaders Licensure Consortium Recommended Standards

The Interstate School Leaders Licensure Consortium (ISLLC) Standards for School Leaders (CCSSO, 1996) are the result of a national initiative to identify unified standards for licensure. The ISLLC standards provide a common vision for effective educational leadership. According to these standards, a school administrator is an educational leader who promotes the success of all students by

- facilitating the development, articulation, implementation, and stewardship of a vision of learning that is shared and supported by the school community;
- advocating, sustaining, and nurturing a school culture and instructional program conducive to student learning and staff professional growth;
- ensuring management of the organization, operations, and resources for a safe, efficient, and effective learning environment;
- collaborating with families and community members, responding to diverse community interests and needs, and mobilizing community resources;
- acting with integrity and fairness and in an ethical manner; and
- understanding, responding to, and influencing the larger political, social, economic, legal, and cultural context. (CCSSO, 1996)

International Society for Technology Education Recommended Standards

Recognizing the need for technology standards for school administrators, the AASA, NSBA, other national school administrator organizations, and the International Society for Technology Education formed a collaborative to develop standards. The standards define the specifics of what superintendents and other school administrators "need to know and be able to do in order to discharge their responsibility as leaders in the effective use of technology in our schools" (TSSA Collaborative, 2001, p. 1). Standards and performance indicators are contained in a framework of six major areas including

- leadership and vision;
- learning and teaching;
- productivity and professional practice;
- support, management, and operations;
- assessment and evaluation; and
- social, legal, and ethical issues.

Comparing the Recommended Standards

Using a framework of administrator skills (Katz, 1955), we compared the four sets of national standards by categorizing the individual standards within each set according to the category of leadership skills required to meet each standard (Figure 3.6).

When preparation programs for superintendents are aligned with these four sets of standards, the development of technical skills and acquiring specialized knowledge are emphasized, as well as the conceptual and human skills that dominate the leadership literature.

The Match between the Superintendent Evaluation Domains and AASA Standards

While the national standards provide a framework for defining the role of the superintendent, it should be noted that the standards tend to reflect generic superintendent duties and responsibilities (DiPaola &

Figure 3.6.   Comparing Leadership Standards

	Technical Skills (special knowledge, tools, and techniques)	Conceptual Skills (ability to see the enterprise as a whole)	Human Skills (working with people, ethical dimensions)
ISLLC Standards (Interstate School Leaders Licensure Consortium)	Organizational management	Ability to develop and sustain culture Ability to develop and implement vision Understand and respond within large context	Collaborations with families and community Integrity and ethical behavior
AASA Standards for the Superintendency (American Association of School Administrators)	Policy and governance Organizational management Curriculum planning Instructional management Human resources management	Leadership and district culture	Communications and community relations Values and ethics
National Technology Standards for School Administrators (TSSA Collaborative)	Curriculum and instruction integrate appropriate technologies Apply technologies to enhance practice and productivity Provide support for integration and infrastructure Plan and implement effective assessments	Create vision for comprehensive integration of technology	Decisions reflect social, legal, ethical, and technology issues
NSBA Key Work (National School Boards Association)	Planning Curriculum alignment, instruction, and assessment focused on standards Accountability	Establish and maintain a positive climate Focus on continuous improvement	Build collaborative relations

Stronge, 2001a). As Carter and Cunningham (1997) noted, the divergent interests and expectations that exist in each school district thwart attempts to standardize criteria for superintendent evaluation. While the standards may only be a general guide, they can be very useful in bringing the board and superintendent together to tailor evaluation criteria to fit the local district (Horler, 1996).

Checklists with details for all eight AASA standards and accompanying indicators are provided in Appendix A. The checklists can be used to assess how well a job description correlates with the AASA standards. Additionally, they can be helpful in aligning a superintendent's evaluation instrument with the standards.

Figure 3.7 depicts the relationship between the recommended superintendent evaluation domains that we identify in this book (Appendix B) and the AASA standards. You will note that we have condensed the AASA standards from eight to six domains for the purposes of designing a performance evaluation system.

Recommended Superintendent Evaluation Domains	AASA Professional Standards							
	Communications and Community Relations	Human Resources Management	Leadership and District Culture	Curriculum Planning and Development	Instructional Management	Policy and Governance	Organizational Management	Values and Ethics of Leadership
Policy and Governance	✓					✓		
Planning and Assessment	✓	✓	✓	✓	✓	✓	✓	
Instructional Leadership	✓		✓	✓	✓	✓		✓
Organizational Management	✓	✓	✓		✓	✓	✓	
Communications and Community Relations	✓		✓	✓		✓	✓	✓
Professionalism	✓		✓			✓		✓

Figure 3.7. Superintendency Matrix Comparing the Recommended Domains and AASA Professional Standards

WHAT IS THE RELATIONSHIP BETWEEN THE SUPERINTENDENT PERFORMANCE STANDARDS AND THE SUPERINTENDENT'S JOB DESCRIPTION?

Local school boards traditionally have defined the responsibilities of the superintendent in terms of a job description—a general description that frequently is related only loosely to actual job responsibilities. Additionally, the job description typically is even more loosely connected to the superintendent's evaluation (DiPaola & Stronge, 2001a, 2001b).

Most superintendents do have a job description, but in *The 2000 Study of the American Superintendency*, only 50.2 percent stated that they are evaluated according to the criteria in the job description (Glass, Bjork, & Brunner, 2000). In our discussion of the superintendent's performance evaluation, what is important is that the job description

- be an accurate general description of the superintendent's role,
- serve as a useful guide in advertising and selecting a superintendent,
- serve as a basis upon which the superintendent's evaluation can be built, and
- be rationally connected to the specific duties and responsibilities contained within the superintendent's performance evaluation.

Figure 3.8 demonstrates the use of language that typically is included in a superintendent job description. We recommend that the school board and superintendent thoughtfully consider the relationship between the job description and the evaluation when developing or revising them. This process is especially important in negotiating a new contract. If the two documents have been properly aligned, it can smooth communications later and help both parties avoid potential misunderstandings.

SUMMARY

In summary, we contend that a comprehensive and productive superintendent evaluation system is founded squarely upon clearly stated and clearly communicated job responsibilities. If the role of the superintendent can be adequately described in the form of performance standards (as presented in Appendix B), then all parties can

- *know* what are the key performance expectations,
- *assess* actual performance based on the standards,
- fairly *judge* success based on objective criteria, and
- make informed *decisions* for improvement.

TITLE: Superintendent of Schools

PRIMARY FUNCTION:
The superintendent of schools provides educational leadership and administers the school district, in compliance with all School Board policies, state codes, and mandates set forth by the State Board of Education through the State Department of Education. The superintendent serves as the chief administrative officer of the school district and is responsible for
  1. General school administration
  2. Instructional programs and services
  3. Personnel leadership and supervision
  4. Business and fiscal operations
  5. School facilities management
  6. Pupil transportation
  7. Record keeping and reporting
  8. Community relations

QUALIFICATIONS:
Possesses certification and qualifications as set forth by the State Board of Education. Possesses professional qualifications and personal attributes as set forth by the School Board.

EVALUATION:
The superintendent shall be evaluated at least annually by the School Board.

AUTHORITY RELATIONSHIPS:
The superintendent of schools is a constitutional state office through which the State Board of Education and Superintendent of Public Instruction exercise their supervision and control of the school district. The superintendent serves as the chief executive officer of the School Board and is responsible for enforcing all board policies. All personnel employed by the School Board answer, through proper channels, to the superintendent of schools.

Figure 3.8.   Sample Superintendent Job Description

REFERENCES

American Association of School Administrators. (1993). *Professional standards for the superintendency.* Arlington, VA: Author.

Carter, G. R., & Cunningham, W. G. (1997). *The American school superintendent: Leading in an age of pressure.* San Francisco: Jossey-Bass.

Council of Chief State School Officers [CCSSO]. (1996). *The interstate school leaders licensure consortium: Standards for school leaders.* Washington, DC: Authors.

DiPaola, M. F., & Stronge, J. H. (2001a). Credible evaluation: Not yet state-of-the-art. *The School Administrator, 58*(2), 18–21.

DiPaola, M. D., & Stronge, J. H. (2001b). Superintendent evaluation in a standards-based environment: A status report from the states. *Journal of Personnel Evaluation in Education, 15*(2), 97–110.

Gemberling, K. W., Smith, C. W., & Villani, J. S. (2000). *The keywork of school boards guidebook.* Alexandria, VA: National School Boards Association.

Glass, T. E., Bjork, L., & Brunner, C. C. (2000). *The 2000 study of the American school superintendency.* Arlington, VA: American Association of School Administrators.

Horler, B. (1996). *A comparison of criteria used in the evaluation of the superintendency in Illinois as perceived by school board presidents and public school superintendents.* Unpublished doctoral dissertation, Northern Illinois University, DeKalb.

Hoyle, J. R., English, F. W., & Steffy, B. E. (1998). *Skills for successful 21st century school leaders: Standards for peak performers.* Arlington, VA: American Association of School Administrators.

Katz, R. L. (1955). Skills of an effective administrator. *Harvard Business Review, 33*(1), 33–42.

Technology Standards for School Administrators Collaborative. (2001). *Technology standards for school administrators (TSSA).* Naperville, IL: North Regional Technology in Education Consortium.

DOCUMENTING THE
SUPERINTENDENT'S PERFORMANCE

As we discussed in chapter 3, the foundation of an effective superintendent performance evaluation system is a comprehensive set of performance standards. However, the set of performance standards alone isn't adequate to ensure a quality evaluation system. While the performance standards describe *what* the superintendent is expected to do, we also need to know *how* the superintendent fulfills her or his work as well as *how well* the work is done. In other words, a quality performance evaluation system will provide ways and means for documenting the superintendent's performance and then offer a rubric for fairly judging that performance.

In this chapter, we explore both the *how* and the *how well* aspects needed for designing and implementing a superintendent performance evaluation system. Specifically, we address the following questions

1. What are appropriate information sources for documenting the superintendent's performance?
2. How can the various information sources be integrated?
3. How is a scoring rubric used?
4. How can a superintendent scoring rubric be helpful in judging the superintendent's effectiveness?

WHAT ARE APPROPRIATE INFORMATION SOURCES FOR DOCUMENTING THE SUPERINTENDENT'S PERFORMANCE?

The role of superintendent requires a performance evaluation system that acknowledges the complexities of the job. It isn't enough to rely on opinion based on limited informal observations and anecdotal evidence. In fact, such an approach to evaluate the superintendent will almost always

- allow uneven influence by a few constituents,
- provide only limited evidence of achievement,
- be based more on speculation than actual performance data,
- be subjective and founded upon opinion, and
- result in an evaluation that is counterproductive to growth and improvement.

In order to develop a complete picture of a superintendent's contribution to the overall success of the school system, the board of education should use multiple broad-based sources of information. These data sources might include informal observations, client surveys, artifacts of performance or portfolios, professional goals, and other relevant sources of information. Systematically documenting performance in a variety of settings using a variety of means enhances the breadth and depth of both the superintendent's and the board's understanding of performance strengths and weaknesses. However, for data sources to be acceptable, they must meet the tests of logic, reliability, fairness, and legality (Peterson, 1995). Answering questions such as the following can assist in determining whether the data sources meet these tests

- Are the data the responsibility of the superintendent?
- Do the data reflect responsibilities included in the superintendent's job description?
- Are the data linked to student learning, leadership, or other key responsibilities reflected in the performance standards?
- Are the data of primary importance in considering the quality of the superintendent's performance?
- Are better data available on the same performance responsibility?

A sound evaluation system will always be based on actual performance data collected through multiple means that are representative of the superintendent's total performance during the period covered by the performance assessment. Thus, using a more comprehensive set of data is essential and can yield a far more valuable performance assessment. Multiple data sources provide for a comprehensive and authentic "performance portrait" of the superintendent's work. The sources of information described in Figure 4.1 provide the most comprehensive and accurate feedback on superintendent performance.

Figure 4.1. Data Sources for Documenting Superintendent Performance

Data Source	Description
Goal Setting and Student Achievement	Superintendents have a definite impact on student learning and academic performance. They set goals for improving student achievement based on appropriate performance measures as part of the strategic planning process.
Document Review	Numerous documents, which are developed in the normal course of events, can be considered as part of the evaluation data collection process.
Client Surveys	Staff and/or selected community members can be insightful for assessing perceptions of clients.
Self-Assessment	Systematic self-reflection and self-assessment can be valuable in the evaluation process, particularly for assisting the superintendent in monitoring achievement and preparing for a more formal evaluation.

HOW CAN THE VARIOUS INFORMATION SOURCES BE INTEGRATED?

Goal Setting and Student Achievement

Despite the emphasis on standards-based education, most ratings of the superintendent's effectiveness bear little relationship to measures of student success and other measurable outcomes. For example, one study (DiPaola & Stronge, 2001) revealed that student achievement currently was used as a criterion for superintendent evaluation in only three states. Nonetheless, if student learning is the stated objective of schooling and if superintendent evaluation is to be linked to student success (see, for example, Mendro, 1998; Stronge & Tucker, 2000; Wright,

Horn, & Sanders, 1997), then it appears reasonable to consider student learning when evaluating superintendents.

When student learning measures are used in the evaluation of superintendents, they must conform to professional standards of practice (Joint Committee on Standards for Educational Evaluation, 1988). While there are numerous pitfalls in the inappropriate and uninformed use of assessment data for evaluation of any sort, particularly for use in personnel evaluation, it is important to maximize the benefits and minimize the liabilities in the connection of student learning and superintendent effectiveness.

School superintendents are the chief school administrators and the leaders of school districts across the nation. The inclusion of "improving student academic progress" as a mandatory standard of superintendent performance highlights the critical role of educational leaders in curriculum planning/development, instructional leadership, and, ultimately, student performance results.

One method to employ in measuring progress for student learning or other worthy goals is the establishment of annual performance goals. These performance goals should be aimed at desirable, yet realistic, improvement targets that are congruent with the school district's needs and/or concerns. Once established, the goals can be reviewed and adjusted as necessary.

With the use of performance goals, the superintendent typically reports progress on achieving the goals at regular intervals throughout the evaluation process. Indicators of goal attainment include documentation via the superintendent's oral and written reports as well as other evidence that can shed light on progress.

Worthy goals can be developed and documented in diverse areas such as

- planning and completing a building program,
- implementing a community relations effort,
- preparing for a bond referendum,
- documenting fiscal management,
- coordinating curriculum development, and
- leading the educational system to increased student progress.

It is important to note, especially if actual measures of student achievement are to be included, that contextual issues beyond the superintendent's control can influence the realization of desired goals. For instance, there are circumstances when the superintendent (or any educator for that matter) does everything possible to enhance student learning, but conditions beyond her or his control prevent maximum benefits for students. Thus, for goals related to student learning, consideration should be given to issues such as student mobility, economic influences on student success, student absenteeism, and other such variables.

Typically, a superintendent and board will jointly establish annual goals focused on improving student achievement, organizational effectiveness, or other worthy endeavors as part of the strategic planning process. Two formats are provided in Appendix C (Superintendent Annual Performance Goals) for developing and assessing annual goals. The goals and the goal fulfillment often are considered to be a primary data source in the superintendent evaluation system.

Document Review

Another important source for obtaining documentation of a superintendent's performance is analysis of artifacts (i.e., the collection of written records and documents produced under the superintendent's auspices as a part of her or his job responsibilities). Artifacts for a superintendent, for example, might include school board meeting minutes, publications written, PowerPoint notes from presentations, agendas from meetings led, record of individuals mentored, and a highlights videotape from press conferences.

A portfolio is a more formal collection of documents—or artifacts—that are useful for demonstrating the performance of the superintendent. Portfolio evaluation involves the systematic collection of data concerning the fulfillment of the duties or responsibilities of the superintendent organized by domains. Some examples of items that may be included in the domain of communications and community relations are newspaper clippings, programs from various events and functions attended, or professional activities/publications. The portfolio provides a forum for dialogue on the full scope of responsibilities for the superintendent's job and provides additional information that may not have been available in any other form.

Client Surveys

In virtually every school district in America, school board members typically receive feedback, often unsolicited, regarding particular programs, events, and efforts of the superintendent and her or his staff. The feedback can come from a telephone call, a casual conversation in the grocery store, or a variety of other informal venues. In the absence of a more systematic method for collecting perceptions of staff and community members, these anecdotal comments form the basis of the board's collective opinion of the superintendent's acceptance and performance as perceived by the school community. In essence, applying client feedback to superintendent performance—albeit informally—is common practice.

In recent years there has been a growing movement for educators to adopt 360-degree assessment principles employed in business and industry, with all segments of the school community having an opportunity to provide feedback data for the evaluation process (see, for example, Manatt, 2000). This client-centered feedback process can provide an avenue for both the superintendent and the board to receive systematic and representative feedback regarding performance. If staff or community perceptions are to be factored into the superintendent's performance evaluation—and they invariably will—then a fairer and more productive approach is to create a formal outlet for receiving that feedback.

A key consideration in collecting data using client surveys is cost. However, the real challenge is to collect survey data so that it meets the tests of logic, reliability, and fairness. Staff and community surveys of a superintendent's various constituents have the potential to provide data that meet the tests if they are well conceived, properly administered, and interpreted fairly. While surveys can provide an important perspective on the superintendent's performance, they should be used as *only one* component in the evaluation system if they are to be employed. Figures 4.2 and 4.3 illustrate how a survey might be designed. Appendix D provides actual sample surveys that can serve as prototypes for developing constituent feedback forms.

Superintendent Self-Evaluation

The process of self-evaluation encourages the superintendent to reflect on personal experience and is closely linked to the goal-setting

_Check One: I am ___ a teacher ___ an administrator ___ a classified employee ___ other_

Superintendent's Name	School District	School Year

Directions: Read the statements about the superintendent. Select the response that best describes your perception and mark each statement in the appropriate column. Comments can be added in the space after the item.

The Superintendent . . .	AGREE	DISAGREE	CANNOT JUDGE
I. Uses effective communication skills.	❑	❑	❑
2. Involves staff members in identifying and meeting school district goals.	❑	❑	❑

Figure 4.2.   Superintendent's Staff Survey Sample Items

process. It also provides a structure for considering future goals and determining strategies for achievement. The self-assessment process is also useful in promoting the superintendent's professional development. Data from self-evaluation may not be objective enough to use in evaluating the superintendent for summative purposes; however, a regular self-evaluation may be very useful in generating dialogue about revealed discrepancies.

Self-assessment can provide a candid preliminary evaluation that the employee may use to determine areas in which improvement is needed. It should be noted that many studies of self-evaluation have revealed that individual educators (as well as other employees) tend to perceive their performance a bit more generously than do their clients. With a basis for comparing her or his perceptions with those of others and interpreting any differences revealed by the comparison,

The Superintendent . . .	AGREE	DISAGREE	CANNOT JUDGE
I. Uses effective communication skills.	❑	❑	❑
2. Involves parents and community members in identifying and meeting school division goals.	❑	❑	❑
3. Communicates a clear vision for the school division.	❑	❑	❑

Figure 4.3.   Superintendent's Community Survey Sample Items

the superintendent would be best prepared if she or he spent time assessing major accomplishments, strengths and weaknesses, reasons for disappointing results, and proposed changes in goals or objectives for the remainder of the current appraisal period or for the next one. Figure 4.4 provides an illustration of a portion of self-evaluation and Appendix E provides a complete self-evaluation form.

DIRECTIONS This form may be used by superintendents in the ongoing self-assessment process. Additionally, it may be well suited for use by superintendents and board members in the interim review or formative evaluation process. Board members may use this form to maintain records throughout the evaluation cycle in preparation for the summative evaluation. Thus, this form serves as a running record for documenting performance of the superintendent from all pertinent data sources. This form should be discussed during evaluation conferences. Place a check in the box when evidence of a performance standard is observed/collected. Make notes in the space provided.

Domain G: Policy and Governance _Performance Standards_	Evidence Noted
G-1. The Superintendent works with the School Board to develop and implement policies that define organizational expectations.	

Comments
_____
_____
_____
_____
_____

Figure 4.4.   Superintendent Self-Assessment

HOW IS A SCORING RUBRIC USED, AND HOW IS IT HELPFUL IN JUDGING THE SUPERINTENDENT'S EFFECTIVENESS?

As described in chapter 3, the domains, job standards, and performance indicators provide a description of well-defined superintendent expectations. After collecting information gathered through goal setting, student performance measures, client surveys, portfolio review, and other appropriate information sources, the evidence needs to be synthesized in order to arrive at a meaningful judgment regarding performance. One tool that can prove most helpful in making evaluation decisions—

whether for formative or summative purposes—is a rating scale—or rubric—against which performance can be assessed.

Rating scales can be designed simply as a dichotomous scale (e.g., acceptable versus unacceptable, meets expectations versus does not meet expectations). However, a more beneficial approach—especially if growth and continuous improvement are key considerations—is a three- or four-point scale that offers opportunities to explain and justify performance ratings. One such example would be the four-point rating scale as illustrated in Figure 4.5.

In this example of a rating scale, four distinct ratings are available for use in assessing the superintendent's performance. The four-point scale enables the board to acknowledge outstanding work quality and

Figure 4.5. Definitions of Terms in Rating Scale

Rating	Definition
Level 4: Performance Exceeds Criteria	Exemplary performance by the superintendent that continually affects students, staff, and programs in the school division in a positive manner.
	For performance to be rated in this category, the performance must consistently exceed the expectations set forth in the performance standards and the board should cite specific examples in a narrative format.
Level 3: Performance Meets Criteria	Performance that consistently meets expectations resulting in quality work in the accomplishment of the job performance standards identified for the superintendent. This is the acceptable performance level that is expected.
Level 2: Performance Requires Improvement	Performance that does not meet standards and requires improvement to produce desired results (i.e., to meet criteria). The board should cite specific evidence in a narrative format (i.e., describe examples of specific behaviors on the part of the superintendent that illustrate the deficiency).
Level 1: Performance Is Unsatisfactory	Unacceptable performance that requires significant improvement to justify continued employment. The board should cite specific evidence in a narrative format (e.g., offering objectively written descriptions of the superintendent's behavior).
Level 0: Cannot Judge	The individual board member does not have enough information to rate performance on an identified standard. (See note below.)

Note: The rating *Cannot Judge* would be used only when an individual board member lacks sufficient information to make a fair or accurate assessment of the superintendent's performance on a specific job standard. However, in the final evaluation, the board would confer and agree on a rating drawn from the review of evidence by the entire board.

An explanation of three- and four-level rating scales appears in Appendix F.

to provide useful feedback for work that is judged to be in need of improvement. Ratings typically are applied to individual performance standards but not to performance indicators. Additionally, ratings can be applied to the domains to provide a more global assessment of performance. Figure 4.6 illustrates how the ratings would be applied in a final evaluation, and Appendix F defines each rating. Appendices G–J offer several sample summative evaluation formats done in both the three-level rating scale and the four-level rating scale.

SUMMARY

In summary, we provided criteria for selecting appropriate information sources for documenting the superintendent's performance. In order to develop a complete picture of a superintendent's contribution to the overall success of the school system, we suggested that the board of education use multiple broad-based sources of information. The advantages of each of the recommended data sources were discussed and methods for integrating them were suggested. Finally, we proposed us-

---

Superintendent's Name _____
Evaluator _____
Academic/Fiscal Year _____

<u>DIRECTIONS</u>
To be completed by the School Board as documentation of the superintendent's evaluation

■ **Domain: Planning and Assessment**

A-1.   The superintendent effectively employs various processes for gathering, analyzing, and using data for decision making.

PERFORMANCE EXCEEDS CRITERIA	PERFORMANCE MEETS CRITERIA	PERFORMANCE REQUIRES IMPROVEMENT	PERFORMANCE IS UNSATISFACTORY	CANNOT JUDGE

Comments:
_____
_____

Figure 4.6.   Sample Superintendent Performance Evaluation Format

ing a rating scale as a tool to make evaluation decisions. Examples of forms and materials related to these chapter elements are provided in the referenced appendixes.

REFERENCES

DiPaola, M. D., & Stronge, J. H. (2001). Superintendent evaluation in a standards-based environment: A status report from the states. *Journal of Personnel Evaluation in Education, 15*(2), 97–110.

Joint Committee on Standards for Educational Evaluation (D. L. Stufflebeam, Chair). (1988). *The personnel evaluation standards: How to assess systems for evaluating educators.* Newbury Park, CA: Corwin Press, Inc.

Manatt, R. P. (2000). Feedback at 360 degrees. *The school administrator web edition.* Available at http://www.aasa.org/publications/sa/2000_10/Manatt.htm.

Mendro, R. L. (1998). Student achievement and school and teacher accountability. *Journal of Personnel Evaluation in Education, 12,* 257–267.

Peterson, K. D. (1995). *Teacher evaluation: A comprehensive guide to new directions and practices.* Thousand Oaks, CA: Corwin Press.

Stronge, J. H., & Tucker, P. D. (2000). *Teacher evaluation and student achievement.* Washington, DC: National Education Association.

Wright, S. P., Horn, S. P., & Sanders, W. L. (1997). Teacher and classroom context effects on student achievement: Implications for teacher evaluation. *Journal of Personnel Evaluation in Education, 11,* 57–67.

5

IMPLEMENTING THE SUPERINTENDENT'S PERFORMANCE EVALUATION

Designing performance standards, selecting sources of data, and creating documents and/or materials for a performance-based assessment of superintendents are critical initial steps. Equally important, however, is the actual implementation of the performance evaluation process.

In this chapter, we provide basic guidelines and suggestions for implementing a superintendent performance evaluation system. Specifically, we address the following questions

- What policy should guide the performance evaluation of the superintendent?
- What procedures should be established?
- What kind of training is required to implement the performance evaluation of the superintendent?

WHAT POLICY SHOULD GUIDE THE PERFORMANCE EVALUATION OF THE SUPERINTENDENT?

Superintendents often remind board members that their job is that of policymakers, not administrators. A board's policy manual should reflect the board's goals and objectives, philosophics, and methods or procedures for handling generic situations. The superintendent's job is to lead the school district within the guidelines set forth in board policy.

Whether or not state law requires it, we recommend that boards evaluate their superintendents annually. Superintendent evaluation is an important responsibility of a school board that should be guided by policy. Policymaking is an opportunity for a board to set the direction and priorities of their school system. In the absence of policy, personal judgment of the superintendent or board members is substituted for clear guidelines established by the board. The result is often inconsistency or unreasonable practice driven by individual agendas or ambiguous goals.

The initiation of policy development begins with recognizing the need for written policy. An annual process as important as evaluating the superintendent creates such a need. Although superintendents are often the initiators of new policy, board members have increasingly shared this responsibility. In the most recent national study of the superintendency (Glass, Bjork, & Brunner, 2000, p. 55), only 42.9 percent of superintendents indicated they originate most policy initiatives.

Policy Components

Both the superintendent and board members should review current policies related to the superintendent including those that govern the evaluation of the superintendent or describe the responsibilities/duties of the superintendent. In the absence of such policy, it is important to initiate policy development. Effective board policy in this area is

- collaboratively developed with the superintendent,
- reflective of the educational goals of the school district,
- written within the scope of the school board's authority,
- inclusive of state requirements for superintendent evaluation,
- good personnel practice,
- adopted through proper board procedure,
- respectful of legal and constitutional rights and requirements,
- congruent with relevant state laws/code, and
- communicated to the person(s) it affects. (McGee, 1988)

The district policy related to superintendent evaluation should reflect the *how, what, when, where,* and *by whom* the process of performance evaluation of the superintendent is to be implemented. Often, the implementation details, actual performance assessment documents and/or forms, and other details may be adopted as addenda or be incorporated into the procedures pursuant to the actual policy. The policy itself should always reflect the board's intentions and beliefs concerning the goals of the process. Typical goals of a policy on superintendent evaluation include

- promoting professional excellence and improving the superintendent's skills;
- clarifying for the superintendent his or her role in the school system as understood by the board of education;
- clarifying the role of superintendent for all board of education members in light of his or her responsibilities, authority, and organizational expectations;
- developing a unified purpose in order to achieve high-priority goals and objectives;
- creating an opportunity for goal achievement through regular appraisal and feedback;
- enhancing organizational health by involving, developing, and strengthening the commitment of individual board members and the superintendent;
- establishing a shared accountability process that improves student achievement;
- assisting the superintendent in improving her or his effectiveness;
- enhancing communication between the board and the superintendent; and
- enhancing communication with the greater school community. (DiPaola & Stronge, 2001a, 2001b; National Education Policy Network of the National School Boards Association, n.d.; Peterson, 1989)

A sample district policy on superintendent evaluation can be found in Appendix K (adapted from New Jersey School Boards Association, 1994).

WHAT PROCEDURES SHOULD BE ESTABLISHED?

The policy should also include or be accompanied by procedures that specify the "nuts and bolts" of the process. We believe that these elements should be clearly identified

1. Evaluation System Components
   - Domains
   - Responsibilities/Standards (employee job expectations)
   - Sample Performance Indicators (typical behaviors for documentation)
   - Rating Scale
   - Behaviorally Anchored Rating Scale or Performance Rubric (provides descriptions of acceptable/unacceptable behavior for each job responsibility)
2. Data Sources (that will be used to document and assess job performance)
   - Formal Observation
   - Informal Observation
   - Student Achievement/Goal Attainment
   - Client Satisfaction (e.g., survey data)
   - Artifact/Portfolio Data
3. Length of the Evaluation Cycle
4. Forms/Materials Used in the Process
   - Summative Evaluation Form
   - Interim Review Form
   - Observation Checklist or Performance Review Form
   - Goal-Setting/Student Achievement Form
   - Data Notebook Guidelines
   - Community Survey/Questionnaire
   - Staff Survey/Questionnaire
   - Improvement Plan Form
5. Training/Staff Development to be Provided
6. Improvement Component for Evaluation System (must be aligned with school system policies/procedures and developed collaboratively with local policymakers):
   - Requirements for Improvement Plan
   - Plan of Action Forms

- Reward/Sanction Plan (e.g., merit increase)
- Staff Development Recommendations Based on Analysis of End-of-Cycle Evaluations (can be part of summative evaluation form)
- Evaluation Report of Year-1 Implementation and Subsequent Revisions

Establishing Procedures

Once the board sets policy, procedures required for full implementation should be developed. Procedures outline the plan for *how* the process will be implemented. Additionally, policies link best to procedures that are

- relevant to the district;
- grounded in solid practice;
- enforceable;
- clear, concise, and concrete;
- taught and retaught through training;
- reviewed and revised periodically; and
- followed by those responsible for implementing the policy.

During the development of procedures, it is important to assess available resources, particularly the amount of time the implementation plan requires to be certain that it meets the *feasibility standard* so the plan can be put into practice. Implementation time includes the time to prepare and train all individuals who participate in the process. Our experience is that the best-designed evaluation process will fail to achieve its goals without the adequate training of all evaluators and evaluatees. Clearly, training is a critical component of the process.

The superintendent evaluation process that has been adopted will generally guide the sequence of implementation. Generally, an *implementation schedule* is developed first. For example, ordinarily the contract year will begin on July 1 and terminate the following June 30. We believe that training all participants is the logical initial step. If goal setting is an element of the process, it should be the next step.

Individual state law or code often requires that the process be completed by a certain date. Figure 5.1 contains a sample *implementation schedule* for a process that includes goal setting, interim review, and a summative review through an entire academic year with a June 30 deadline. In some states the process must be completed by the end of April if the board has intentions of terminating employment. In some states the process has an early spring deadline regardless of the board's intention. A schedule with an April 30 deadline is in column two of Figure 5.1. This sample implementation schedule assumes a contract with the superintendent that would continue employment into the next year.

An implementation schedule creates a real ongoing process in which all parties know when each regular meeting is scheduled during the process. We suggest that regular executive board meeting agendas actually reflect the evaluation sessions as agenda items. This is critical since experience tells us that the most common course of action is to use time for other "pressing" issues. Not adhering to the implementation schedule undermines the process and creates an evaluation "event," the summative evaluation, at the end of the year.

Figure 5.1. Implementation Schedule

Summative by		
June 30th	April 30th	Activity
July	July	Provide training opportunities for all participants in the process
Prior to August 15	Prior to June 1	Board establishes annual district goals
Prior to September 1	Prior to July 1	Superintendent meets with board to set his or her annual goal(s)
Prior to November 15	Prior to October 15	Superintendent meets with board to discuss progress made on goal attainment and receives feedback on overall performance
Prior to January 31	Prior to January 1	Superintendent meets with board to discuss progress made on goal attainment and receives feedback on overall performance via an *Interim Review* document
Prior to April 15	Prior to March 15	Superintendent meets with board to discuss progress made on goal attainment and receive feedback on overall performance
Prior to June 30	Prior to April 30	Superintendent meets with board to discuss the annual *Summative Evaluation*

WHAT KIND OF TRAINING IS REQUIRED TO IMPLEMENT THE PERFORMANCE EVALUATION OF THE SUPERINTENDENT?

Whenever a new superintendent evaluation process is adopted, training must be provided for board members as well as the superintendent. The absence of adequate training places board members in a frustrating, uncomfortable position; they should fully participate in the superintendent's evaluation, yet they do not have a clear understanding of their individual roles or of how to implement the process. When a disconnect between superintendent evaluation policy and actual implementation occurs, it undermines the intent and goals of the process, often resulting in judgments of performance grounded only in personal perceptions.

In our national study of superintendent evaluation, we found that of the criteria for quality personnel evaluation, the standard most often absent was *accuracy*. The accuracy standard requires valid, reliable, and systematic data free from bias. Since school board members are not always trained adequately to complete evaluations to meet this criterion, the fairness of evaluations is a serious issue. In the state of Alabama, a trained state evaluator actually conducts the evaluation of the superintendent for each board, but this is not common practice. Several states require training of new board members and most of the state AASA or NSBA affiliates provide information related to guidelines for good evaluations. Although several state school board associations indicate that training is offered to school board members, the frequency and extent of the training varies. And, since turnover in the ranks of school board members can be high, it is critically important that new members be trained adequately to evaluate superintendents.

We strongly suggest that the training program be designed to include these components for both superintendents and board members

- orientation/overview,
- application/implementation guidelines,
- establishment of student achievement and other goals,
- collection of documents/artifacts,
- use of documents/artifacts for evaluation,
- use of student achievement data for evaluation,

- legal requirements for evaluation, and
- conferencing skills.

We advocate for the superintendent's and the entire board's participation in all phases of the evaluation process. Some school boards also elect to use an outside facilitator to assist with the superintendent's evaluation. If an outside facilitator is employed for this purpose, the facilitator should be trained in the process and meet with the superintendent and board jointly to clarify roles. Additionally, the superintendent's participation, cooperation, and support are critical.

After the annual performance evaluation is complete, we suggest that the board issue a statement during a public board meeting explaining the process and goals, as well as whatever action(s) the board has taken. The superintendent should be publicly commended whenever appropriate.

SUMMARY

A board's responsibility as policymaker includes crafting a policy, regulations, and procedures for a quality performance evaluation system for all employees, including the superintendent. Once consensus is reached on the goals of the process, policy can begin to guide

- development and adoption of a comprehensive evaluation process;
- policies that specify details of the process;
- procedures and timelines for implementation; and
- training of board members, the superintendent, and any other participant.

Evaluating the performance of the superintendent is one of the most critical tasks of board members and should be undertaken with the same regard for planning and professionalism that is employed in selecting a superintendent. Quality evaluations enable superintendents to know which aspects of her or his performance the board feels are working well and which need improvement. The process helps establish priorities in goal setting for the next evaluation cycle and should include commendations for accomplishments as well as recommendations for improvement. Regular and systematic evaluation enhances communication and the relationship between the board and the superintendent.

REFERENCES

DiPaola, M. F., & Stronge, J. H. (2001a). Credible evaluation: Not yet state-of-the-art. *The School Administrator, 58*(2), 18–21.

DiPaola, M. D., & Stronge, J. H. (2001b). Superintendent evaluation in a standards-based environment: A status report from the states. *Journal of Personnel Evaluation in Education, 15*(2), 97–110.

Glass, T. E., Bjork, L., & Brunner, C. C. (2000). *The study of the American school superintendency: A look at the superintendent of education in the new millennium.* Arlington, VA: American Association of School Administrators.

McGee, M. (1988). *School board evaluation: A comprehensive self-help guide.* Alexandria, VA: National School Boards Association.

National Education Policy Network of the National School Boards Association. (n.d.). *Evaluation of the superintendent.* Alexandria, VA: Author.

New Jersey School Boards Association. (1994). *Sample district policy evaluation of the chief school administrator.* Trenton, NJ: Author.

Peterson, D. (1989). *Superintendent evaluation.* ERIC Digest Series Number EA 42. Eugene, OR: ERIC Clearinghouse on Educational Management.

6

WHERE DO WE GO FROM HERE?

This era of accountability and standards-based reform has created a focus on performance-based assessment for all school professionals, including the superintendent. Unfortunately, within this high-stakes environment, local political pressures can often result in a deteriorating working relationship between the board and the superintendent. This downwardly spiraling working relationship is too frequently expressed in terms of community dissatisfaction and conflict that, in turn, results in the election of new board members running on a platform that includes replacing the superintendent. Poor communication between the superintendent and the board leads to mistrust. Conflict results and unfortunately, reason disappears (Hoyle & Skrla, 1999). Within this context, accountability is a double-edged sword that cuts to the heart of two critical issues: fair and unbiased evaluation of superintendent performance and superintendent job security. In this chapter, we discuss the impact of a sound superintendent evaluation system and provide some direction for action. In particular, we address the following questions

- What should superintendents and school boards do to adopt a state-of-the-art superintendent evaluation process?
- How does a process of superintendent evaluation support the changes necessary to effect continuous improvement?

- How does a process of superintendent evaluation enhance the achievement of district goals?

WHAT SHOULD SUPERINTENDENTS AND SCHOOL BOARDS DO TO ADOPT A STATE-OF-THE-ART SUPERINTENDENT EVALUATION PROCESS?

A logical first step is to define criteria for a performance evaluation. The evaluation criteria recommended in this document may be modified or used as is by local school boards to achieve that goal. They are urged to carefully consider their organizational goals and review their policy on evaluation before proceeding with a review of their evaluation system and criteria. Policy should reflect organizational goals. System goals should shape the job descriptions for all employees within the district, including the superintendent. Using job descriptions as a starting point, the evaluation criteria we offer can be used to further define the expectations of school superintendents.

Superintendents should consider the evaluation process when negotiating initial and subsequent contracts. "The language governing evaluation in the superintendent's contract of employment can certainly serve to enhance the evaluation process" (Finkelstein, 2002, p. 2). For example, a provision stating that the superintendent receive a copy of all forms used during the process by individual board members may provide a more realistic reflection of actual superintendent performance. Since the interim and summative evaluation forms reflect a composite of individual board member's judgments, they may be more subjective, reflecting the sentiments of the individual(s) who prepares those documents. The contract should also guarantee the right of the superintendent to respond to the evaluation in writing and make the response a permanent attachment to the summative document.

Evaluation as a Process Not an Event

All too often superintendent evaluations are performed hurriedly at the last moment in an attempt to satisfy a legal requirement or a policy mandate. If the evaluation is merely an *event* it has little, if any, impact on the professional growth of the superintendent or improvement of the school district. Superintendent evaluation, when implemented as a continuous *process*, is a valuable tool that enhances communication, keeps the respective parties informed, and provides opportunities for mutual understanding, growth, and development. Only when board members and the superintendent engage in an ongoing process can the critical responsibility of the board to evaluate the superintendent be satisfactorily met.

Evaluation Timeline

There are several "natural" times for the board to examine its current practice and modify it by adopting a *process* of superintendent evaluation. They include

- while planning for an evaluation process development during the last quarter of a school year in order to begin implementation of the process the following year;
- prior to the retirement/departure of a superintendent in order to reassess and refine expectations and the job description before a search for a successor begins; and
- while working with an interim superintendent.

A superintendent should be included in the development phase in order for the board to get her or his perspective.

We have provided a suggested *implementation schedule* for evaluation in chapter 5 (see Figure 5.1). Adopting such a schedule and placing quarterly meetings for the purpose of the evaluation on the board's regular meeting agenda is a first step in implementing this *process*. These scheduled meetings provide time for the superintendent to apprise the board of progress made on established goal(s), as well as opportunities for the board members to provide feedback to the superintendent about her or his performance. The time invested in the evaluation *process* has the potential to yield positive outcomes for all parties involved, as well as the entire school district. The schedule also creates a cycle of evaluation in which a summative evaluation at the end of the *process* provides guidance for goal setting at the beginning of the next evaluation cycle (see Figure 6.1).

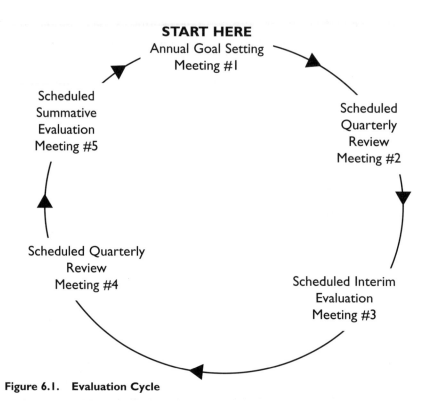

Figure 6.1. Evaluation Cycle

Implementing the Process

In using the guidelines to develop a new superintendent evaluation system

1. Review guidelines for consistency with local policy for superintendent evaluation and stated purposes of evaluation, criteria, and
   descriptors based on job descriptions.
2. Modify evaluation criteria and descriptors to reflect local goals, job
   descriptions, and priorities.
3. Select information collection strategies, such as
   - observations,
   - client, staff, and community surveys,
   - review of documents/evidence of performance,
   - goal statements and evidence of achievement,
   - measures of student learning, and
   - miscellaneous sources (e.g., knowledge of professional contri-
     butions, community support).

4. Create a schedule for information collection and evaluation reports, such as
   - number and timing of information collection strategies and
   - calendar for administering evaluation system with deadlines for evaluation summaries.
5. Establish a rating scale for judging performance, including
   - choice of terms and
   - definition of terms.
6. Define a performance improvement process for professional educators identified as needing remedial assistance.
7. Develop necessary guidelines and forms, including
   - observation forms,
   - client survey forms,
   - interim evaluation forms,
   - summative evaluation forms, and
   - improvement assistance plan.

We have provided complete guidelines for use in modifying an existing evaluation system. In using the guidelines to modify an existing superintendent evaluation system

- review the guidelines for consistency with local policy for superintendent evaluation, stated purposes of evaluation, and content of current evaluation criteria;
- make modifications to the existing evaluation system based on the requirements of applicable state laws/code, guidelines, and local needs; and
- give special consideration to the integration of student learning measures in the evaluative criteria.

WHAT ARE THE BENEFITS OF SUPERINTENDENT EVALUATION FOR A SCHOOL DISTRICT AND SUPERINTENDENT?

Meeting the demands for increased effectiveness of schools cannot occur without systemic change. One of the benefits of implementing an evaluation system like the one we've recommended is that it facilitates the necessary process of change. Innovative solutions are necessary for school districts to improve the achievement of all students. This change process has created a more complex role for superintendents and board members. No longer are they able to rely on traditional ways of thinking and working a task at a time. Doing so would prevent them from envisioning the future, enticing others to participate in making that vision a reality, and creating a climate for learning.

The evaluation process can help sustain focus on systemic change initiatives. The primary goal of school districts is improving achievement for all students (Gemberling, Smith, & Villani, 2000). Implicit in this focus on continuous improvement is the need to monitor, assess, and modify. In the evaluation process, school boards set annual goals for the district. The goals for the superintendent and all other employees must support and reflect the district goals. Think of the old and venerable adage, "What gets measured, gets done." It is through this evaluation process that the achievement of goals is monitored and "measured." Those responsible for goal achievement are motivated to work to meet the challenges because they know their progress will be "measured." Through this accountability, the changes necessary to improve student achievement have a better chance of being sustained.

Another benefit of the process of superintendent evaluation is that it provides valuable feedback on the quality of performance. As a result, superintendents and other employees have information to plan individual professional growth and development endeavors that have direct connections to expectations of their performance. This changes the traditional "one size fits all" professional development models and connects development activities directly to performance expectations. It makes professional growth and development a responsibility of both the superintendent and the board.

HOW DOES A PROCESS OF SUPERINTENDENT EVALUATION ENHANCE THE ACHIEVEMENT OF DISTRICT GOALS?

We hope we have made a compelling case to convince school boards and superintendents to embrace and adopt a comprehensive performance-based assessment process to evaluate chief school administrators. This collaborative process should

- provide clear expectations,
- use multiple data sources,
- require regular communication,
- provide useful feedback to superintendents on the quality of their performance,
- provide the constructive feedback necessary for superintendents to responsibly plan for their own professional growth and development, and
- assist school board members and the superintendent in staying focused on the goals they set to help students achieve at higher levels.

Superintendents should help their school boards use the resources we have provided to design and implement a sound process to assess the superintendent's performance. In the design phase, mutually agree on what outcomes you would like the process to yield. The process must include performance criteria grounded in the real expectations of the board and community. As these evolve or change it is important to adjust the evaluation criteria accordingly. Doing so maintains a fair, reasonable, state-of-the-art superintendent evaluation system.

The increasing expectations of and demands on the superintendent and board members often create an environment in which there never seems to be enough time to adequately address all of the issues. Time constraints cause board members and superintendents to struggle with proactively planning for the future. All too often one of the issues that is shortchanged is evaluating the superintendent. We urge local school boards to recognize their responsibilities in providing a fair, comprehensive evaluation of their superintendents based on reliable and valid data. They should make the development of a performance-based evaluation process a priority.

We are confident that job satisfaction, communication, and working relationships will be enhanced when a comprehensive behavior-based performance assessment process is used to evaluate the superintendent. Such a process will help the superintendent improve her or his performance and help the school board fulfill its responsibilities. If we can use superintendent evaluation positively and proactively, we can improve the quality of our schools and, ultimately, the success of our students.

REFERENCES

Finkelstein, B. (2002, June). Evaluating the superintendent. In *On Target* (newsletter). Trenton, NJ: New Jersey Association of School Administrators.
Gemberling, K. W., Smith, C. W., & Villani, J. S. (2000). *The keywork of school boards guidebook.* Alexandria, VA: National School Board Association.
Hoyle, J. R., & Skrla, L. (1999). The politics of superintendent evaluation. *Journal of Personnel Evaluation in Education, 13*(4), 405–419.

Appendix A

AMERICAN ASSOCIATION OF SCHOOL ADMINISTRATORS (AASA) STANDARDS AND INDICATORS

Directions for use: These standards and indicators may be used as a guide in comparing the school district's current evaluation framework to the American Association of School Administrator's recommendations. The user may check "Y" for yes or "N" for no to note whether the indicator is part of the evaluation system.

STANDARD 1: LEADERSHIP AND DISTRICT CULTURE

INDICATORS	Y	N
Formulate a written vision statement of future direction for the district		
Demonstrate an awareness of international issues affecting schools and students		
Promote academic rigor and excellence for staff and students		
Maintain personal, physical, and emotional wellness		
Empower others to reach high levels of performance		
Build self-esteem in staff and students		
Exhibit creative problem solving		
Promote and model risk taking		
Respect and encourage diversity among people and programs		
Manage time effectively		
Facilitate comparative planning between constituencies		
Conduct district school climate assessments		
Exhibit multicultural and ethnic understanding		
Promote the value of understanding and celebrating school community cultures		

STANDARD 2: POLICY AND GOVERNANCE

INDICATORS	Y	N
Describe the system of public school governance in our democracy		
Describe procedures for superintendent–board of education interpersonal and working relationships		
Formulate a district policy for external and internal programs		
Relate local policy to state and federal regulations and requirements		
Describe procedures to avoid civil and criminal liabilities		

STANDARD 3: COMMUNICATIONS AND COMMUNITY RELATIONS

INDICATORS	Y	N
Articulate district vision, mission, and priorities to the community and mass media		
Demonstrate an understanding of political theory and skills needed to build community support for district priorities		
Understand and be able to communicate with all cultural groups in the community		
Demonstrate that good judgment and actions communicate as well as words		
Develop formal and informal techniques to gain external perception of a district by means of surveys, advisory groups, and personal contact		
Communicate and project an articulate position for education		
Write and speak clearly and forcefully		
Demonstrate formal and informal listening skills		
Demonstrate group membership and leadership skills		
Identify the political forces in a community		
Identify the political context of the community environment		
Formulate strategies for passing referenda		
Persuade the community to adopt an initiative for the welfare of students		
Demonstrate conflict mediation		
Demonstrate consensus building		
Demonstrate school/community relations, school-business partnerships, and related public service activities		
Identify, track, and deal with issues		
Develop and carry out internal and external communication plans		

STANDARD 4: ORGANIZATIONAL MANAGEMENT

INDICATORS	Y	N
Define processes for gathering, analyzing, and using data for informed decision making		
Demonstrate a problem-framing process		
Define the major components of quality management		
Develop, implement, and monitor change processes to build capacities to serve clients		
Discuss legal concepts, regulations, and codes for school operations		
Describe the process of delegating responsibility for decision making		
Develop a process for maintaining accurate fiscal reporting		
Acquire, allocate, and manage human, material, and financial resources to effectively and accountably ensure successful student learning		
Use technological applications to enhance administration of business and support systems		
Demonstrate financial forecasting, planning, and cash flow management		
Perform budget planning, management, account auditing, and monitoring		
Demonstrate a grasp of practices in administering auxiliary programs, such as maintenance, facilities, food services, etc.		
Demonstrate planning and scheduling of personal time and organization work		

STANDARD 5: CURRICULUM PLANNING AND DEVELOPMENT

INDICATORS	Y	N
Develop core curriculum design and delivery systems for diverse school communities		
Describe curriculum planning/futures methods to anticipate occupational trends and their educational implication for lifelong learners		
Demonstrate an understanding of instructional taxonomies, goals, objectives, and processes		
Describe cognitive development and learning theories and their importance to the sequencing of instruction		
Demonstrate an understanding of child and adolescent growth and development		
Describe a process to create developmentally appropriate curricula and instructional practices for all children and adolescents		
Demonstrate the use of computers and other technologies in educational programming		
Conduct assessments of present and future student learning needs		
Develop a process for faculty input in continued and systematic renewal of the curriculum to ensure appropriate scope, sequence, and content		
Demonstrate an understanding of curricular alignment to ensure improved student performance and higher order thinking		

STANDARD 6: INSTRUCTIONAL MANAGEMENT

INDICATORS	Y	N
Develop, implement, and monitor change processes to improve student learning, adult development, and climates for learning		
Demonstrate an understanding of motivation in the instructional process		
Describe classroom management theories and techniques		
Demonstrate an understanding of the development of the total student, including the physical, social, emotional, cognitive, and linguistic needs		
Formulate a plan to assess appropriate teaching methods and strategies for all learners		
Analyze available instructional resources and assign them in the most cost-effective and equitable manner to enhance student outcomes		
Describe instructional strategies that include the role of multicultural sensitivity and diverse learning styles		
Exhibit applications of computer technology connected to instructional programs		
Describe how to interpret and use testing/assessment results to improve education		
Demonstrate knowledge of research findings on the use of a variety of instructional strategies		
Describe a student achievement monitoring and reporting system		

STANDARD 7: HUMAN RESOURCES MANAGEMENT

INDICATORS	Y	N
Develop a plan to assess system and staff needs to identify areas for concentrated staff development		
Demonstrate knowledge of adult learning theory and motivation		
Evaluate the effectiveness of comprehensive staff development programming to determine its effect on professional performance		
Demonstrate use of system and staff evaluation data for personnel policy and decision making		
Monitor and improve organizational health/morale		
Demonstrate personnel management strategies		
Understand alternative benefit packages		
Assess individual and institutional sources of stress and develop methods for reducing stress (e.g., counseling, exercise programs, and diet)		
Demonstrate knowledge of personnel services and categorical programs		

STANDARD 8: VALUES AND ETHICS OF LEADERSHIP

INDICATORS	Y	N
Exhibit multicultural and ethnic understanding and sensitivity		
Describe the role of schooling in a democratic society		
Demonstrate ethical and personal integrity		
Model accepted moral and ethical standards in all interactions		
Describe a strategy to promote the value that moral and ethical practices are established and practiced in each classroom and school in a free and democratic society		
Describe a strategy to ensure that diversity of religion, ethnicity, and way of life in the district are respected		
Formulate a plan to coordinate social, health, and other community agencies for the support of each child in the district		

Appendix B

RECOMMENDED SUPERINTENDENT DOMAINS, PERFORMANCE STANDARDS, AND PERFORMANCE INDICATORS

SUPERINTENDENT DOMAINS

Domain G: Policy and Governance
Domain A: Planning and Assessment
Domain L: Instructional Leadership
Domain M: Organizational Management
Domain C: Communications and Community Relations
Domain P: Professionalism

SUPERINTENDENT EVALUATION CRITERIA: DOMAINS, PERFORMANCE STANDARDS, AND PERFORMANCE INDICATORS

Domain G: Policy and Governance

Performance Standard G-1

The Superintendent works with the school board to develop and implement policies that define organizational expectations. The superintendent . . .

- supports and enforces all school board policies and informs all constituents of changes to the school board policies.
- recommends changes to the school board when school board policies conflict with the school board's vision for education.
- develops administrative regulations that support the application of school board policies.
- recommends policies and procedures that protect the security and integrity of the district infrastructure and the data it contains.
- recommends policies and procedures that protect the rights and confidentiality of staff and students.
- maintains/improves relations between the superintendent and school board through periodic joint seminars, workshops, and training sessions.

Performance Standard G-2

The superintendent functions as the primary instructional leader for the school district, relying on support from staff as necessary when advising the school board. The superintendent . . .

- involves staff as necessary when planning/providing recommendations to the school board.
- demonstrates professional and personal skills, which facilitate staff involvement.
- responds directly and factually to the school board.
- demonstrates tact when offering recommendations.

Performance Standard G-3

The superintendent oversees the administration of the school district's day-to-day operations. The superintendent . . .

- explores/applies operational methods, which enable the school district to apply resources in an efficient manner.
- keeps the school board informed on needs and issues confronting school district employees.
- informs the school board of actions that require school board involvement.

- delegates authority and responsibility to other employees as needs/ opportunities arise.

Performance Standard G-4

The superintendent works with all individuals, groups, agencies, committees, and organizations to provide and maintain schools that are safe and productive. The superintendent . . .

- ensures safe, secure schools for all students and employees.
- proposes improvements to school facilities, increasing public confidence and trust that schools are safe and effective learning environments.
- uses technology to enhance professional practices and increase productivity.

Domain A: Planning and Assessment

Performance Standard A-1

The superintendent effectively employs various processes for gathering, analyzing, and using data for decision making. The superintendent . . .

- applies current research related to effective techniques for gathering data from individuals, groups, programs, and the community.
- uses reliable data in making decisions.
- reviews analyses of student academic achievement through standardized test results and other academic sources.
- provides staff with data in a collaborative effort to determine needs for improvement.
- applies and communicates statistical findings to identify strengths and weaknesses in programs and practices in order to ensure continuous improvement.
- plans and implements changes in programs and/or curricula based on data.
- reviews annual analyses of district's test and subtest scores by school and discipline in order to assess school improvement and monitor improvement plans.

- develops, monitors, and assesses district and school improvement plans.

Performance Standard A-2

The superintendent organizes the collaborative development and implementation of a district strategic plan based on analysis of data from a variety of sources. The superintendent . . .

- provides leadership in the development of a shared vision for educational improvement and of a strategic plan to attain that vision.
- implements strategies for the inclusion of staff and various stakeholders in the planning process.
- supports the district's mission by identifying, articulating, and planning to meet the educational needs of students, staff, and other stakeholders.
- works collaboratively to develop long- and short-range goals and objectives consistent with the strategic plan and monitors progress in achieving long- and short-range goals and objectives.
- provides feedback to principals on goal achievement and needs for improvement.
- supports staff through the stages of the change process.
- maintains stakeholders' focus on long-range mission and goals throughout the implementation process.

Performance Standard A-3

The superintendent plans, implements, supports, and assesses instructional programs that enhance teaching and student achievement of the state educational standards. The superintendent . . .

- demonstrates a working knowledge and understanding of the state educational standards and district curricular requirements.
- supports the development of a comprehensive curriculum utilizing goals and objectives in alignment with the state educational standards.

- oversees the planning, implementation, evaluation, and revision of the curriculum on a systematic and ongoing basis.
- provides resources and materials to accomplish instructional goals for all students.
- facilitates programs/curricular changes to meet state or federal requirements.
- monitors and assesses the effect of the programs and/or curricula on student achievement.

Performance Standard A-4

The superintendent develops plans for effective allocation of fiscal and other resources. The superintendent . . .

- acquires, allocates, and manages district resources in compliance with all laws to ensure the effective and equitable support of all of the district's students, schools, and programs.
- allocates resources consistent with the mission and strategic plan of the district.
- meets and works collaboratively with the board and appropriate staff to determine priorities for budgeting and for the effective allocation of space and human resources.
- utilizes human and material resources outside the district that may support and/or enhance the achievement of goals and objectives.
- provides adequate staffing and other resources to support technology infrastructure and integration across the school district.
- monitors/assesses resource allocation and revises allocation plans based on implementation data.
- oversees budget development and prepares it for school board approval.
- implements the annual school operating budget and capital improvement plan.
- applies financial forecasting and planning procedures that support efficient use of all school district resources.
- maintains appropriate and accurate financial records.

Domain L: Instructional Leadership

Performance Standard L-1

The superintendent communicates a clear vision of excellence and continuous improvement consistent with the goals of the school district. The superintendent . . .

- demonstrates personal commitment to achieving the mission of the school district.
- articulates a shared vision to all constituencies and ensures that staff members are working in concert with the district's strategic plan.
- informs members of the board and community of current research related to best practices in curriculum and instruction.
- explores, disseminates, and applies knowledge and information about new or improved methods of instruction or related issues.
- shares evaluation data and subsequent plans for continuous improvement with staff, students, and other stakeholders.
- recognizes, encourages, and celebrates excellence among staff and students.
- demonstrates strong motivation and high standards and models self-evaluation.
- fosters positive morale and team spirit.

Performance Standard L-2

The superintendent oversees the alignment, coordination, and delivery of assigned programs and/or curricular areas. The superintendent . . .

- articulates curricular goals, objectives, and frameworks to staff and other stakeholders.
- works with staff to develop a written plan for the coordination and articulation of curricular goals.
- works with the board, staff, and community representatives to identify needs and determine priorities regarding program delivery.

- provides direction and support in planning and implementing activities and programs consistent with continuous improvement efforts and attainment of instructional goals.
- monitors coordination of instructional programs with state and local standards.
- facilitates the effective coordination and integration of district curricular and cocurricular programs.
- reviews an annual analysis of the school vision's test and subtest scores by school and discipline in order to assess and monitor school improvement.
- demonstrates an understanding of occupational trends and their educational implications.

Performance Standard L-3

The superintendent selects, inducts, supports, evaluates, and retains quality instructional and support personnel. The superintendent . . .

- maintains and disseminates a current handbook of personnel policies and procedures.
- establishes and uses selection procedures that ensure fairness and equity in selecting the best candidates.
- makes recommendations regarding personnel decisions consistent with established policies and procedures.
- oversees the recruitment, appointment, induction, and assignment of the most qualified personnel available.
- establishes and implements formal and informal induction procedures to promote assistance for and acceptance of new employees.
- sets high standards for staff performance.
- evaluates performance of personnel consistent with district policies, provides formal and informal feedback, and maintains accurate evaluation records.
- recommends the reappointment and/or promotion of competent, effective personnel.
- provides support and resources for staff to improve job performance and recognizes and supports the achievements of highly effective staff members.

Performance Standard L-4

The superintendent provides staff development programs consistent with program evaluation results and school instructional improvement plans. The superintendent . . .

- leads the development and implementation of a systematic professional development plan for individuals, including members of the board, and for the district.
- works collaboratively with members of the staff in using student achievement data to determine relevant professional development opportunities.
- meets with principals regularly to assess ongoing school improvement efforts.
- evaluates the effectiveness of the professional development plan in relation to district goals.
- encourages participation in relevant conferences, course work, and activities of professional organizations.
- shares program evaluation results and demonstrates connection of results to ongoing staff development efforts.
- supports staff participation in internal and external professional development opportunities as appropriate.

Performance Standard L-5

The superintendent identifies, analyzes, and resolves problems using effective problem-solving techniques. The superintendent . . .

- identifies and addresses problems in a timely and effective manner.
- demonstrates fairness in identifying multiple points of view around problem situations.
- involves stakeholders in analyzing problems and developing solutions.
- monitors implementation of problem resolutions.
- provides shared leadership and decision-making opportunities for staff that promote a climate of collaboration and collegiality.
- delegates responsibility appropriately to staff members.
- maintains focus on school and district mission and goals.
- promotes an atmosphere of mutual respect and courtesy.

Performance Standard L-6

The superintendent assesses factors affecting student achievement and serves as an agent of change for needed improvements. The superintendent . . .

- makes appropriate changes in the curriculum and scheduling.
- optimizes available physical resources.
- adjusts placement of students.
- adjusts personnel assignments.
- provides appropriate training for instructional personnel.

Performance Standard L-7

The superintendent ensures that curricular design, instructional strategies, and learning environments integrate appropriate technologies to maximize student learning. The superintendent . . .

- provides equitable access for students and staff to technologies that facilitate productivity and enhance learning.
- communicates expectations that technology will be used to increase student achievement.
- ensures that budget priorities reflect a focus on technology as it relates to enhanced learning.
- Provides technology-rich learning experiences for all students.

Domain M: Organizational Management

Performance Standard M-1

The superintendent actively supports a safe and positive environment for students and staff. The superintendent . . .

- facilitates the implementation of sound, research-based theories and techniques of classroom management, student discipline, and school safety to ensure a safe, orderly environment conducive to teaching and learning.
- clearly communicates expectations regarding behavior to students, staff, parents, and other members of the community.

- clearly communicates procedures for handling disciplinary problems.
- implements and enforces school district code of conduct and appropriate disciplinary policies and procedures in a timely and consistent manner.
- supports effective programs through which students develop self-discipline and conflict resolution skills.
- calmly and effectively manages emergency situations as they occur.
- is proactive in addressing potential problem situations.
- consistently conveys mutual respect, concern, and high expectations to students, staff, parents, and community members.
- recognizes students and staff for their academic, cocurricular, personal, and professional achievements.

Performance Standard M-2

The superintendent develops procedures for working with the board of education that define mutual expectations, working relationships, and strategies for formulating district policies. The superintendent . . .

- respects the policymaking authority and responsibility of the board.
- develops and uses a systematic means of keeping members of the board informed with complete, accurate information.
- facilitates the delineation of superintendent and board roles and the articulation of mutual expectations.
- recommends policy additions and/or modifications to improve student learning and district effectiveness.
- anticipates future needs and demonstrates a bias for action.
- values group interaction and problem solving.
- expresses opinions on policy issues directly to the board.
- supports and implements policy established by the board.

Performance Standard M-3

The superintendent effectively manages human, material, and financial resources to ensure student learning and to comply with legal mandates. The superintendent . . .

- complies with federal, state, and local statutes, regulations, policies, and procedures.
- collaboratively plans and prepares a fiscally responsible budget to support the organization's mission and goals.
- demonstrates effectiveness in obtaining necessary resources.
- establishes and uses accepted procedures for receiving and disbursing funds.
- ensures that expenditures are within limits approved by the board.
- implements appropriate management techniques and group processes to define roles, delegate activities and responsibilities, and determine accountability for goal attainment.
- prepares and implements short- and long-range plans for facilities and sites.
- ensures proper maintenance and repair of district property and equipment.
- monitors any construction, renovation, or demolition of district buildings.
- regularly reports to the board on the financial condition of the district.
- monitors the efficient use of resources.
- works with staff to establish an effective schedule for use of shared resources.
- ensures the maintenance of accurate personnel records.

Performance Standard M-4

The superintendent demonstrates effective organizational skills to achieve school, community, and district goals. The superintendent . . .

- demonstrates and communicates a working knowledge and understanding of school district policies and procedures.
- ensures compliance and follow-through regarding policies and procedures.
- uses time to the best advantage, manages scheduling effectively, and follows tasks to completion.
- employs appropriate technologies to communicate, manage schedules and resources, assess performance, and enhance learning.
- performs duties in an accurate and timely manner.

- maintains appropriate and accurate records.
- efficiently and appropriately prioritizes and addresses multiple issues and projects.
- systematically evaluates progress on achieving established goals.
- keeps the board, staff, and community apprised of progress in achieving the district's goals.

Performance Standard M-5

The superintendent implements sound personnel procedures in recruiting, employing, and retaining the best qualified and most competent teachers, administrators, and other personnel. The superintendent . . .

- knows and follows proper procedures for staffing.
- recruits and assigns the best available personnel in terms of personal and professional competence.
- establishes and uses selection procedures that ensure fairness and equity in selecting the best candidates for employment and promotions.
- establishes and implements formal and informal induction procedures for new employees.
- assigns and transfers employees as the needs of the school district dictate and reports such information to the school board.

Performance Standard M-6

The superintendent provides staff development for all categories of personnel consistent with individual needs, program evaluation results, and instructional improvement plans. The superintendent . . .

- oversees the planning and evaluation of the staff development program.
- works collaboratively with members of the staff in using student achievement data to identify relevant professional development needs.
- encourages and supports employee participation in appropriate internal and external development opportunities.
- maintains an emphasis on technological fluency and provides staff development opportunities to support high expectations.

Performance Standard M-7

The superintendent plans and implements a systematic employee performance evaluation system. The superintendent . . .

- establishes a fair and meaningful employee evaluation system that promotes high expectations of all staff.
- establishes evaluation procedures that assess demonstrated growth in achieving technology standards.
- provides training for all administrative and supervisory personnel in the evaluation and documentation of teacher and administrative performance that includes student achievement as a criterion.
- provides for positive recognition of identified strengths and accomplishments.
- provides assistance to employees requiring remediation.
- provides oversight in the identification of strengths and weaknesses of employees, formal and informal feedback, and dismissal of ineffective employees.
- provides an annual report to the school board summarizing the results of employee evaluations.

Domain C: Communications and Community Relations

Performance Standard C-1

The superintendent promotes effective communication and interpersonal relations within the school district. The superintendent . . .

- promotes a climate of trust and teamwork within the district.
- facilitates constructive and timely communication.
- initiates communication and facilitates cooperation among staff regarding curriculum or program initiatives.
- establishes a culture that encourages responsible risk taking while requiring accountability for results.
- models professionally appropriate communication skills, interpersonal relations, and conflict mediation.
- maintains visibility and accessibility to staff.
- solicits staff input to discuss issues and goals and to promote effective decision making.

- establishes and maintains a collaborative relationship with staff members in promoting the district's mission and in communicating expectations.

Performance Standard C-2

The superintendent establishes and maintains effective channels of communication with board members and between the schools and community, strengthening support of constituencies and building coalitions. The superintendent . . .

- accepts responsibility for maintaining communication between the board and district personnel.
- anticipates, analyzes, and discusses emerging educational/district issues with the board on a regular basis.
- systematically provides accurate, relevant information to the board to facilitate decision making.
- establishes, maintains, and evaluates a planned, two-way system of communication with community constituencies.
- communicates school and district goals, objectives, and expectations to stakeholders.
- is politically astute and demonstrates the skills necessary to build community support for district goals and priorities.
- works cooperatively with representatives of the news media.
- establishes partnerships with public and private agencies to enhance the district's ability to serve students and other constituents.
- uses acceptable written and oral language.

Performance Standard C-3

The superintendent works collaboratively with staff, families, and community members to secure resources and to support the success of a diverse student population. The superintendent . . .

- is responsive to the conditions and dynamics of the diversity within the school community.
- treats people with respect.

- models and promotes multicultural awareness, gender sensitivity, and the appreciation of diversity in the community.
- is knowledgeable about laws regarding individual and group rights and responsibilities and scrupulously avoids actions that might violate them.
- collaborates with staff, families, and community leaders and responds to identified needs of individual students and groups of students.
- promotes the value of understanding and celebrating school/community cultures.

Performance Standard C-4

The superintendent creates an atmosphere of trust and mutual respect with staff and community. The superintendent . . .

- unites people toward a common goal.
- fosters an environment conducive to the teaching and learning process.
- promotes collaboration and collegiality among the staff.
- treats all personnel fairly without favoritism or discrimination while demanding high-performance standards.

Domain P: Professionalism

Performance Standard P-1

The superintendent models professional, moral, and ethical standards as well as personal integrity in all interactions. The superintendent . . .

- understands and models appropriate value systems, ethics, and moral leadership.
- promotes the establishment and application of moral and ethical practices in each school and classroom.
- relates to board members, staff, and others in an ethical and professional manner.
- maintains the physical and emotional wellness necessary to meet the responsibilities of the position.

- serves as an articulate spokesperson for the school district and represents the district favorably at the local, state, and national levels.
- resolves concerns and problems in an appropriate manner.
- respects and maintains confidentiality and assumes responsibility for personal actions and those of subordinates.
- maintains a professional demeanor and appearance appropriate to responsibilities.
- demonstrates good character and integrity.

Performance Standard P-2

The superintendent works in a collegial and collaborative manner with school personnel and the community to promote and support the mission and goals of the school district. The superintendent . . .

- demonstrates flexibility and a collaborative attitude in supporting professionals/other staff/work teams.
- supports the district and advances its mission/goals.
- establishes and supports a district culture that encourages collaboration and teamwork in achieving goals.
- maintains effective working relationships with other administrators and staff.
- shares ideas and information and considers the interests and needs of staff members and community stakeholders in promoting and supporting district goals and services.

Performance Standard P-3

The superintendent takes responsibility for and participates in a meaningful and continuous process of professional development that results in the enhancement of student learning. The superintendent . . .

- participates in professional growth activities, including conferences, workshops, course work, and/or membership in professional organizations at the district, state, and/or national levels.
- evaluates and identifies areas of personal strength and weakness related to providing district leadership.

- sets goals for improvement of skills and professional performance.
- maintains a high level of personal knowledge regarding new developments and techniques, including technology, and shares the information with appropriate staff.
- comprehends and applies current research on educational issues, trends, and practices.
- networks with colleagues to share knowledge about effective educational practices and to improve and enhance administrative knowledge, skills, and organizational success.
- maintains proper licensure and certification.

Performance Standard P-4

The superintendent provides service to the profession, the district, and the community. The superintendent . . .

- serves on district, state, and/or national committees and maintains an active role in professional organizations.
- contributes to and supports the development of the profession by serving as an instructor, mentor, coach, presenter, researcher, or supervisor.
- organizes, facilitates, and presents at local, state, and/or national conferences.
- supports and participates in efforts to align district goals and activities with community endeavors.

Appendix C

SUPERINTENDENT ANNUAL
PERFORMANCE GOALS

■ **SAMPLE I** ■

Superintendent Annual Performance Goals

Superintendent _____ Evaluator_____

Academic/Fiscal Year _____ School District _____

Goal/Objective:						
Indicators of Success	Superintendent's Assessment					Board Assessment
	Achieved	Partially Achieved	Not Achieved	Agree	Disagree	Comments

■ SAMPLE II (2 pages) ■

Superintendent Annual Performance Goals

Superintendent: **Academic Year:**

Focus *[The area/topic to be addressed (e.g., student learning, school safety)]*

Baseline Data *[status at beginning of year]*

Goal Statement *[desired result(s)]*

Board Members' Signatures/Date

■ SAMPLE II (2 Pages) ■

Superintendent Annual Performance Goals

Timeline for Goal Achievement *[quarterly progress report]*

Quarter	Benchmarks (target expectation by given date)	Activities	Interim Results (achieved results by given date)	Board Member Initials
October 1				
January 1				
April 1				
June 30				

Appendix D

STAFF AND COMMUNITY SURVEYS

Suggestions for use: After receiving the surveys back, make a tally chart by question of the responses. Look for areas where stakeholders are recognizing strengths and identifying weaknesses. The survey results may serve as one of the multiple forms of evidence of a superintendent's effectiveness as the results demonstrate how the stakeholders perceive the superintendent.

■ **Superintendent** ■

Community Survey

Check One: I am a ___ *parent* ___ *community member* ___ *public official* ___ *other*

_____   _____   _____
Superintendent's Name   School District   School Year

Directions: Read the statements about the superintendent. Select the response that best describes your perception and mark each statement in the appropriate column. Comments can
be added in the space after the item or on the back.

The Superintendent . . .

	AGREE	DISAGREE	CANNOT JUDGE
1. Uses effective communication skills	❏	❏	❏
2. Involves parents and community members in identifying and meeting school district goals	❏	❏	❏
3. Communicates a clear vision for the school district	❏	❏	❏
4. Seeks to obtain community support for school district goals	❏	❏	❏
5. Relates to all people in a courteous and professional manner	❏	❏	❏
6. Supports community activities	❏	❏	❏
7. Aligns school district goals with community needs	❏	❏	❏
8. Communicates and supports clear and consistent expectations for student behavior	❏	❏	❏
9. Is approachable and accessible to parents and other community members	❏	❏	❏
10. Applies policies and regulations in a fair and consistent manner	❏	❏	❏
11. Is a positive ambassador for the school district	❏	❏	❏
12. Handles emergency situations appropriately	❏	❏	❏
13. Is responsive to the needs of all constituencies/cultures in our community	❏	❏	❏
14. Ensures well-maintained facilities that meet program/demographic requirements	❏	❏	❏
15. Shares student assessment data and improvement plans with parents and other community members	❏	❏	❏
16. Shares district assessment data with parents and other stakeholders	❏	❏	❏
17. Resolves problems and concerns in an appropriate manner	❏	❏	❏
18. Recognizes and encourages excellence among students and staff	❏	❏	❏
19. Ensures student/school safety	❏	❏	❏
20. Keeps me informed about school district programs and goals	❏	❏	❏

Thank you for your feedback.

■ Superintendent ■

Staff Survey

Check One: I am a ___ teacher ___ an administrator ___ a classified employee ___ other

Superintendent's Name	School District	School Year

Directions: Read the statements about the superintendent. Select the response that best describes your perception and mark each statement in the appropriate column. Comments can be added in the space after the item.

The Superintendent . . .

	AGREE	DISAGREE	CANNOT JUDGE
1. Uses effective communication skills	❑	❑	❑
2. Involves staff members in identifying and meeting school district goals	❑	❑	❑
3. Communicates a clear vision for the school district	❑	❑	❑
4. Seeks to obtain staff and community support for school district goals and priorities	❑	❑	❑
5. Relates to all constituencies in a courteous and professional manner	❑	❑	❑
6. Supports school and community activities	❑	❑	❑
7. Aligns school district goals with community needs and priorities	❑	❑	❑
8. Communicates and supports clear and consistent expectations for student behavior	❑	❑	❑
9. Is approachable and accessible	❑	❑	❑
10. Applies policies and regulations in a fair and consistent manner	❑	❑	❑
11. Is a positive ambassador for the school district	❑	❑	❑
12. Handles emergency situations in a calm and appropriate manner	❑	❑	❑
13. Uses sound financial management practices	❑	❑	❑
14. Is responsive to the needs of all constituencies/ cultures in our community	❑	❑	❑
15. Ensures well-maintained facilities that meet program/demographic requirements	❑	❑	❑
16. Shares student assessment data and improvement plans with staff	❑	❑	❑
17. Delegates responsibility effectively and appropriately	❑	❑	❑
18. Provides direction and support for instruction	❑	❑	❑
19. Demonstrates a commitment to students	❑	❑	❑
20. Resolves problems and concerns in an appropriate manner	❑	❑	❑
21. Recognizes and encourages excellence among students and staff	❑	❑	❑
22. Ensures student/school safety	❑	❑	❑
23. Encourages teamwork and collaboration	❑	❑	❑

	AGREE	DISAGREE	CANNOT JUDGE
24. Conducts meetings that are meaningful and productive	❏	❏	❏
25. Shares district assessment data and improvement plans with staff	❏	❏	❏
26. Is approachable and accessible to staff	❏	❏	❏
27. Maintains high standards of ethics, honesty, and integrity	❏	❏	❏
28. Encourages and supports professional growth and development that meet district needs and priorities	❏	❏	❏
29. Distributes resources equitably and efficiently	❏	❏	❏

Thank you for your feedback.

Appendix E

SELF-ASSESSMENT, PERFORMANCE CHECKLIST, AND INTERIM REVIEW

■ **Superintendent** ■

Self-Assessment / Performance Checklist / Interim Review

Superintendent's Name _____

Evaluator _____

Academic/Fiscal Year _____

DIRECTIONS This form may be used by superintendents in the ongoing self-assessment process. Additionally, it may be well suited for use by superintendents and board members in the interim review or formative evaluation process. Board members may use this form to maintain records throughout the evaluation cycle in preparation for the summative evaluation. Thus, this form serves as a running record for documenting performance of the superintendent from all pertinent data sources. This form should be discussed during evaluation conferences. Place a check in the box when evidence of a performance standard is observed/collected. Make notes in the space provided.

Domain G: Policy and Governance *Performance Standards*	Evidence Noted
G-1. The superintendent works with the school board to develop and implement policies that define organizational expectations. *Notes*	
G-2. The superintendent functions as the primary instructional leader for the school district, relying on support from staff as necessary when advising the school board. *Notes*	
G-3. The superintendent oversees the administration of the school district's day-to-day operations. *Notes*	
G-4. The superintendent works with all individuals, groups, agencies, committees, and organizations to provide and maintain schools that are safe and productive. *Notes*	

Additional Notes

_____
_____
_____

Domain A: Planning and Assessment *Performance Standards*	Evidence Noted
A-1. The superintendent effectively employs various processes for gathering, analyzing, and using data for decision making. *Notes*	
A-2. The superintendent organizes the collaborative development implementation of a district strategic plan based on analysis of data from a variety of sources. *Notes*	
A-3. The superintendent plans, implements, supports, and assesses instructional programs that enhance teaching and student achievement of the state educational standards. *Notes*	
A-4. The superintendent develops plans for effective allocation of fiscal and other resources. *Notes*	

Domain L: Instructional Leadership *Performance Standards*	Evidence Noted
L-1. The superintendent communicates a clear vision of excellence and continuous improvement consistent with the goals of the school district. *Notes*	
L-2. The superintendent oversees the alignment, coordination, and delivery of assigned programs and/or curricular areas. *Notes*	
L-3. The superintendent selects, inducts, supports, evaluates, and retains quality instructional and support personnel. *Notes*	
L-4. The superintendent provides staff development programs consistent with program evaluation results and school instructional improvement plans. *Notes*	
L-5. The superintendent identifies, analyzes, and resolves problems using effective problem-solving techniques. *Notes*	
L-6. The superintendent assesses factors affecting student achievement and serves as an agent of change for needed improvements. *Notes*	

Additional Notes

Domain M: Organizational Management *Performance Standards*	Evidence Noted
M-1. The superintendent actively supports a safe and positive environment for students and staff. *Notes*	
M-2. The superintendent develops procedures for working with the board of education that define mutual expectations, working relationships, and strategies for formulating district policies. *Notes*	
M-3. The superintendent effectively manages human, material, and financial resources to ensure student learning and to comply with legal mandates. *Notes*	
M-4. The superintendent demonstrates effective organizational skills to achieve school, community, and district goals. *Notes*	
M-5. The superintendent implements sound personnel procedures in recruiting, employing, and retaining the best qualified and most competent teachers, administrators, and other personnel. *Notes*	
M-6. The superintendent provides staff development for all categories of personnel consistent with individual needs, program evaluation results, and instructional improvement plans. *Notes*	
M-7. The superintendent plans and implements a systematic employee performance evaluation system. *Notes*	

Domain C: Communications & Community Relations *Performance Standards*	Evidence Noted
C-1. The superintendent promotes effective communication and interpersonal relations within the school district. *Notes*	
C-2. The superintendent establishes and maintains effective channels of communication with board members and between the schools and community, strengthening support of constituencies and building coalitions. *Notes*	
C-3. The superintendent works collaboratively with staff, families, and community members to secure resources and to support the success of a diverse student population. *Notes*	
C-4. The superintendent creates an atmosphere of trust and mutual respect with staff and community. *Notes*	

Domain P: Professionalism *Performance Standards*	Evidence Noted
P-1. The superintendent models professional, moral, and ethical standards as well as personal integrity in all interactions. *Notes*	
P-2. The superintendent works in a collegial and collaborative manner with school personnel and the community to promote and support the mission and goals of the school district. *Notes*	
P-3. The superintendent takes responsibility for and participates in a meaningful and continuous process of professional development that results in the enhancement of student learning. *Notes*	
P-4. The superintendent provides service to the profession, the district, and the community. *Notes*	

Summary

Strengths

Areas for Improvement

_____ Recommend continued employment in current position
_____ Requires action/intervention plan for improvement [ATTACH PLAN]
_____ Recommend continued employment but not in current position
_____ Recommend dismissal

Signatures:

_____   _____
Superintendent/Date   Evaluator/Date

EMPLOYEE SIGNATURE ACKNOWLEDGES RECEIPT OF THIS FORM. WRITTEN COMMENTS MAY BE ATTACHED.
COMMENTS ATTACHED: __YES _ NO

Appendix F

SUPERINTENDENT SUMMATIVE EVALUATION

EXPLANATION OF RATING SCALE

There are two major considerations in assessing job performance during summative evaluation: the actual standards and how well they are performed. The domains, performance standards, and performance indicators provide a description of well-defined superintendent expectations. Appendix B provides guidelines for assessment.

After collecting information gathered through goal achievement, observation, student performance measures, review of artifacts, and other appropriate sources, the Board would use a three- or four-point rating scale to evaluate performance of superintendent standards. The rating scale provides a description of different levels of how well the duties (i.e., standards) are performed on a continuum from "exceeds expectations" to "unsatisfactory." The use of the four-level rating scale enables School Board members to acknowledge effective performance (i.e., "exceeds expectations" and "meets expectations") and provides two levels of feedback for superintendents not meeting expectations (i.e., "needs improvement" and "unsatisfactory"). The three-level rating scale enables Board members to acknowledge effective performance (i.e., "exceeds expectations" and "meets expectations") and provides one level of feedback for superintendents not meeting expectations ("has not met expectations.")

Ratings are applied either to domains or individual standards, but not to performance indicators. The following sections define the various rating levels, provide detailed information on the performance of standards for improvement purposes, and describe the decision-making process for assessing performance.

4-Level Rating Scale

Rating	Definition
Exceeds Criteria / Expectations	The superintendent surpasses required standards, consistently producing exemplary work that optimizes district goals and priorities.
Meets Criteria / Expectations	The performance of the superintendent consistently fulfills standards resulting in quality work that affects district goals and priorities in a positive manner. *This rating is a high performance standard and is expected of all superintendents.*
Needs Improvement / Requires Assistance	The superintendent inconsistently meets standards resulting in less than quality work performance where district goals and priorities need improvement.
Unsatisfactory	The superintendent does not adequately fulfill responsibilities, resulting in inferior work performance and negatively influencing district goals and priorities.

3-Level Rating Scale

Rating	Definition
Exceeds Criteria / Expectations	The superintendent surpasses required standards, consistently producing exemplary work that optimizes district goals and priorities.
Meets Criteria / Expectations	The performance of the superintendent consistently fulfills standards resulting in quality work that affects district goals and priorities in a positive manner. *This rating is a high performance standard and is expected of all superintendents.*
Has Not Met Expectations	The superintendent inconsistently or has not adequately met the standards, resulting in less than quality work.

Appendix G

SAMPLE
SUMMATIVE EVALUATION FORM I

■ 4-level rating scale (9 pages) ■

Superintendent Summative Evaluation

Superintendent's Name _____
Evaluator _____
Academic/Fiscal Year _____

<u>DIRECTIONS</u>
To be completed by the School Board as documentation of the superintendent's evaluation.

■ Domain G: Policy and Governance

Performance Standards

G-1. The superintendent works with the school board to develop and implement policies that define organizational expectations.

PERFORMANCE EXCEEDS CRITERIA	PERFORMANCE MEETS CRITERIA	PERFORMANCE REQUIRES IMPROVEMENT	PERFORMANCE IS UNSATISFACTORY	CANNOT JUDGE

Comments:
_____
_____

G-2. The superintendent functions as the primary instructional leader for the school district, relying on support from staff as necessary when advising the school board.

PERFORMANCE EXCEEDS CRITERIA	PERFORMANCE MEETS CRITERIA	PERFORMANCE REQUIRES IMPROVEMENT	PERFORMANCE IS UNSATISFACTORY	CANNOT JUDGE

Comments:
_____
_____

G-3. The superintendent oversees the administration of the school district's day-to-day operations.
Comments:
_____
_____

PERFORMANCE EXCEEDS CRITERIA	PERFORMANCE MEETS CRITERIA	PERFORMANCE REQUIRES IMPROVEMENT	PERFORMANCE IS UNSATISFACTORY	CANNOT JUDGE

Comments:
_____
_____

G-4. The superintendent works with all individuals, groups, agencies, committees, and organizations to provide and maintain schools that are safe and productive.

PERFORMANCE EXCEEDS CRITERIA	PERFORMANCE MEETS CRITERIA	PERFORMANCE REQUIRES IMPROVEMENT	PERFORMANCE IS UNSATISFACTORY	CANNOT JUDGE

Comments:

_____

_____

■ Domain A: Planning and Assessment

Performance Standards

A-1. The superintendent effectively employs various processes for gathering, analyzing, and using data for decision making.

PERFORMANCE EXCEEDS CRITERIA	PERFORMANCE MEETS CRITERIA	PERFORMANCE REQUIRES IMPROVEMENT	PERFORMANCE IS UNSATISFACTORY	CANNOT JUDGE

Comments:

_____

_____

A-2. The superintendent organizes the collaborative development and implementation of a district strategic plan based on analysis of data from a variety of sources.

PERFORMANCE EXCEEDS CRITERIA	PERFORMANCE MEETS CRITERIA	PERFORMANCE REQUIRES IMPROVEMENT	PERFORMANCE IS UNSATISFACTORY	CANNOT JUDGE

Comments:

_____

_____

A-3. The superintendent plans, implements, supports, and assesses instructional programs that enhance teaching and student achievement of the state educational standards.

PERFORMANCE EXCEEDS CRITERIA	PERFORMANCE MEETS CRITERIA	PERFORMANCE REQUIRES IMPROVEMENT	PERFORMANCE IS UNSATISFACTORY	CANNOT JUDGE

Comments:

_____

_____

A-4. The superintendent develops plans for effective allocation of fiscal and other
      resources.

PERFORMANCE EXCEEDS CRITERIA	PERFORMANCE MEETS CRITERIA	PERFORMANCE REQUIRES IMPROVEMENT	PERFORMANCE IS UNSATISFACTORY	CANNOT JUDGE

Comments:

_____

_____

■ Domain L: Instructional Leadership

Performance Standards

L-1. The superintendent communicates a clear vision of excellence and continuous
      improvement consistent with the goals of the school district.

PERFORMANCE EXCEEDS CRITERIA	PERFORMANCE MEETS CRITERIA	PERFORMANCE REQUIRES IMPROVEMENT	PERFORMANCE IS UNSATISFACTORY	CANNOT JUDGE

Comments:

_____

_____

L-2. The superintendent oversees the alignment, coordination, and delivery of assigned
      programs and/or curricular areas.

PERFORMANCE EXCEEDS CRITERIA	PERFORMANCE MEETS CRITERIA	PERFORMANCE REQUIRES IMPROVEMENT	PERFORMANCE IS UNSATISFACTORY	CANNOT JUDGE

Comments:

_____

_____

L-3. The superintendent selects, inducts, supports, evaluates, and retains quality instructional
      and support personnel.

PERFORMANCE EXCEEDS CRITERIA	PERFORMANCE MEETS CRITERIA	PERFORMANCE REQUIRES IMPROVEMENT	PERFORMANCE IS UNSATISFACTORY	CANNOT JUDGE

Comments:

_____

_____

L-4. The superintendent provides staff development programs consistent with the program evaluation results and school instructional improvement plans.

PERFORMANCE EXCEEDS CRITERIA	PERFORMANCE MEETS CRITERIA	PERFORMANCE REQUIRES IMPROVEMENT	PERFORMANCE IS UNSATISFACTORY	CANNOT JUDGE

Comments:
_____
_____

L-5. The superintendent identifies, analyzes, and resolves problems using effective problem-solving techniques.

PERFORMANCE EXCEEDS CRITERIA	PERFORMANCE MEETS CRITERIA	PERFORMANCE REQUIRES IMPROVEMENT	PERFORMANCE IS UNSATISFACTORY	CANNOT JUDGE

Comments:
_____
_____

L-6. The superintendent assesses factors affecting student achievement and serves as an agent of change for needed improvements.

PERFORMANCE EXCEEDS CRITERIA	PERFORMANCE MEETS CRITERIA	PERFORMANCE REQUIRES IMPROVEMENT	PERFORMANCE IS UNSATISFACTORY	CANNOT JUDGE

Comments:
_____
_____

■ Domain M: Organizational Management

Performance Standards

M-1. The superintendent actively supports a safe and positive environment for students and staff.

PERFORMANCE EXCEEDS CRITERIA	PERFORMANCE MEETS CRITERIA	PERFORMANCE REQUIRES IMPROVEMENT	PERFORMANCE IS UNSATISFACTORY	CANNOT JUDGE

Comments:
_____
_____

M-2. The superintendent develops procedures for working with the board of education
      that define mutual expectations, working relationships, and strategies for formulating
      district policies.

PERFORMANCE EXCEEDS CRITERIA	PERFORMANCE MEETS CRITERIA	PERFORMANCE REQUIRES IMPROVEMENT	PERFORMANCE IS UNSATISFACTORY	CANNOT JUDGE

Comments:

_____

_____

M-3. The superintendent effectively manages human, material, and financial resources to
      ensure student learning and to comply with legal mandates.

PERFORMANCE EXCEEDS CRITERIA	PERFORMANCE MEETS CRITERIA	PERFORMANCE REQUIRES IMPROVEMENT	PERFORMANCE IS UNSATISFACTORY	CANNOT JUDGE

Comments:

_____

_____

M-4. The superintendent demonstrates effective organizational skills to achieve school,
      community, and district goals.

PERFORMANCE EXCEEDS CRITERIA	PERFORMANCE MEETS CRITERIA	PERFORMANCE REQUIRES IMPROVEMENT	PERFORMANCE IS UNSATISFACTORY	CANNOT JUDGE

Comments:

_____

_____

M-5. The superintendent implements sound personnel procedures in recruiting, employing,
      and retaining the best qualified and most competent teachers, administrators, and
      other personnel.

PERFORMANCE EXCEEDS CRITERIA	PERFORMANCE MEETS CRITERIA	PERFORMANCE REQUIRES IMPROVEMENT	PERFORMANCE IS UNSATISFACTORY	CANNOT JUDGE

Comments:

_____

_____

M-6.   The superintendent provides staff development for all categories of personnel consistent with individual needs, program evaluation results, and instructional improvement plans.

PERFORMANCE EXCEEDS CRITERIA	PERFORMANCE MEETS CRITERIA	PERFORMANCE REQUIRES IMPROVEMENT	PERFORMANCE IS UNSATISFACTORY	CANNOT JUDGE

Comments:
_____
_____

M-7.   The superintendent plans and implements a systematic employee performance evaluation system.

PERFORMANCE EXCEEDS CRITERIA	PERFORMANCE MEETS CRITERIA	PERFORMANCE REQUIRES IMPROVEMENT	PERFORMANCE IS UNSATISFACTORY	CANNOT JUDGE

Comments:
_____
_____

■ Domain C: Communications and Community Relations

Performance Standards

C-1.   The superintendent promotes effective communication and interpersonal relations within the school district.

PERFORMANCE EXCEEDS CRITERIA	PERFORMANCE MEETS CRITERIA	PERFORMANCE REQUIRES IMPROVEMENT	PERFORMANCE IS UNSATISFACTORY	CANNOT JUDGE

Comments:
_____
_____

C-2.   The superintendent establishes and maintains effective channels of communication with board members and between the schools and community, strengthening support of constituencies and building coalitions.

PERFORMANCE EXCEEDS CRITERIA	PERFORMANCE MEETS CRITERIA	PERFORMANCE REQUIRES IMPROVEMENT	PERFORMANCE IS UNSATISFACTORY	CANNOT JUDGE

Comments:
_____
_____

C-3.   The superintendent works collaboratively with staff, families, and community members to secure resources and to support the success of a diverse student population.

PERFORMANCE EXCEEDS CRITERIA	PERFORMANCE MEETS CRITERIA	PERFORMANCE REQUIRES IMPROVEMENT	PERFORMANCE IS UNSATISFACTORY	CANNOT JUDGE

Comments:

_____

_____

C-4.   The superintendent creates an atmosphere of trust and mutual respect with staff and community.

PERFORMANCE EXCEEDS CRITERIA	PERFORMANCE MEETS CRITERIA	PERFORMANCE REQUIRES IMPROVEMENT	PERFORMANCE IS UNSATISFACTORY	CANNOT JUDGE

Comments:

_____

_____

■ Domain P: Professionalism

Performance Standards

P-1.   The superintendent models professional, moral, and ethical standards as well as personal integrity in all interactions.

PERFORMANCE EXCEEDS CRITERIA	PERFORMANCE MEETS CRITERIA	PERFORMANCE REQUIRES IMPROVEMENT	PERFORMANCE IS UNSATISFACTORY	CANNOT JUDGE

Comments:

_____

_____

P-2.   The superintendent works in a collegial and collaborative manner with school personnel and the community to promote and support the mission and goals of the school district.

PERFORMANCE EXCEEDS CRITERIA	PERFORMANCE MEETS CRITERIA	PERFORMANCE REQUIRES IMPROVEMENT	PERFORMANCE IS UNSATISFACTORY	CANNOT JUDGE

Comments:

_____

_____

P-3. The superintendent takes responsibility for and participates in a meaningful and continuous process of professional development that results in the enhancement of student learning.

PERFORMANCE EXCEEDS CRITERIA	PERFORMANCE MEETS CRITERIA	PERFORMANCE REQUIRES IMPROVEMENT	PERFORMANCE IS UNSATISFACTORY	CANNOT JUDGE

Comments:

P-4. The superintendent provides service to the profession, the district, and the community.

PERFORMANCE EXCEEDS CRITERIA	PERFORMANCE MEETS CRITERIA	PERFORMANCE REQUIRES IMPROVEMENT	PERFORMANCE IS UNSATISFACTORY	CANNOT JUDGE

Comments:

■ Evaluation Summary ■

■ Strengths

■ Areas for Improvement

Signatures:

_____   _____
Superintendent   School Board Chair

_____   _____
Date   Date

SUPERINTENDENT'S SIGNATURE ACKNOWLEDGES RECEIPT OF THIS FORM.
WRITTEN COMMENTS MAY BE ATTACHED.
COMMENTS ATTACHED: _____ YES _____ NO

■ 3-level rating scale (9 pages) ■

Superintendent Summative Evaluation

Superintendent's Name _____

Evaluator _____

Academic/Fiscal Year _____

<u>DIRECTIONS</u>
To be completed by the School Board as documentation of the superintendent's evaluation.

■ Domain G: Policy and Governance

Performance Standards

G-1. The superintendent works with the school board to develop and implement policies that define organizational expectations.

PERFORMANCE EXCEEDS CRITERIA	PERFORMANCE MEETS CRITERIA	HAS NOT MET PERFORMANCE CRITERIA	CANNOT JUDGE

Comments:

_____

_____

G-2. The superintendent functions as the primary instructional leader for the school district, relying on support from staff as necessary when advising the school board.

PERFORMANCE EXCEEDS CRITERIA	PERFORMANCE MEETS CRITERIA	HAS NOT MET PERFORMANCE CRITERIA	CANNOT JUDGE

Comments:

_____

_____

G-3. The superintendent oversees the administration of the school district's day-to-day operations.

PERFORMANCE EXCEEDS CRITERIA	PERFORMANCE MEETS CRITERIA	HAS NOT MET PERFORMANCE CRITERIA	CANNOT JUDGE

Comments:

_____

_____

G-4. The superintendent works with all individuals, groups, agencies, committees, and organizations to provide and maintain schools that are safe and productive.

PERFORMANCE EXCEEDS CRITERIA	PERFORMANCE MEETS CRITERIA	HAS NOT MET PERFORMANCE CRITERIA	CANNOT JUDGE

Comments:

_____

_____

■ Domain A: Planning and Assessment

Performance Standards

A-1. The superintendent effectively employs various processes for gathering, analyzing, and using data for decision making.

PERFORMANCE EXCEEDS CRITERIA	PERFORMANCE MEETS CRITERIA	HAS NOT MET PERFORMANCE CRITERIA	CANNOT JUDGE

Comments:

_____

_____

A-2. The superintendent organizes the collaborative development and implementation of a district strategic plan based on analysis of data from a variety of sources.

PERFORMANCE EXCEEDS CRITERIA	PERFORMANCE MEETS CRITERIA	HAS NOT MET PERFORMANCE CRITERIA	CANNOT JUDGE

Comments:

_____

_____

A-3. The superintendent plans, implements, supports, and assesses instructional programs that enhance teaching and student achievement of the state educational standards.

PERFORMANCE EXCEEDS CRITERIA	PERFORMANCE MEETS CRITERIA	HAS NOT MET PERFORMANCE CRITERIA	CANNOT JUDGE

Comments:

_____

_____

A-4. The superintendent develops plans for effective allocation of fiscal and other resources.

PERFORMANCE EXCEEDS CRITERIA	PERFORMANCE MEETS CRITERIA	HAS NOT MET PERFORMANCE CRITERIA	CANNOT JUDGE

Comments:

_____

_____

■ Domain L: Instructional Leadership

Performance Standards

L-1. The superintendent communicates a clear vision of excellence and continuous improvement consistent with the goals of the school district.

PERFORMANCE EXCEEDS CRITERIA	PERFORMANCE MEETS CRITERIA	HAS NOT MET PERFORMANCE CRITERIA	CANNOT JUDGE

Comments:

_____

_____

L-2. The superintendent oversees the alignment, coordination, and delivery of assigned programs and/or curricular areas.

PERFORMANCE EXCEEDS CRITERIA	PERFORMANCE MEETS CRITERIA	HAS NOT MET PERFORMANCE CRITERIA	CANNOT JUDGE

Comments:

_____

_____

L-3. The superintendent selects, inducts, supports, evaluates, and retains quality instructional and support personnel.

PERFORMANCE EXCEEDS CRITERIA	PERFORMANCE MEETS CRITERIA	HAS NOT MET PERFORMANCE CRITERIA	CANNOT JUDGE

Comments:

_____

_____

L-4. The superintendent provides staff development programs consistent with the program evaluation results and school instructional improvement plans.

PERFORMANCE EXCEEDS CRITERIA	PERFORMANCE MEETS CRITERIA	HAS NOT MET PERFORMANCE CRITERIA	CANNOT JUDGE

Comments:
_____
_____

L-5. The superintendent identifies, analyzes, and resolves problems using effective problem-solving techniques.

PERFORMANCE EXCEEDS CRITERIA	PERFORMANCE MEETS CRITERIA	HAS NOT MET PERFORMANCE CRITERIA	CANNOT JUDGE

Comments:
_____
_____

L-6. The superintendent assesses factors affecting student achievement and serves as an agent of change for needed improvements.

PERFORMANCE EXCEEDS CRITERIA	PERFORMANCE MEETS CRITERIA	HAS NOT MET PERFORMANCE CRITERIA	CANNOT JUDGE

Comments:
_____
_____

■ Domain M: Organizational Management

Performance Standards

M-1. The superintendent actively supports a safe and positive environment for students and staff.

PERFORMANCE EXCEEDS CRITERIA	PERFORMANCE MEETS CRITERIA	HAS NOT MET PERFORMANCE CRITERIA	CANNOT JUDGE

Comments:
_____
_____

M-2.   The superintendent develops procedures for working with the board of education that define mutual expectations, working relationships, and strategies for formulating district policies.

PERFORMANCE EXCEEDS CRITERIA	PERFORMANCE MEETS CRITERIA	HAS NOT MET PERFORMANCE CRITERIA	CANNOT JUDGE

Comments:

_____

_____

M-3.   The superintendent effectively manages human, material, and financial resources to ensure student learning and to comply with legal mandates.

PERFORMANCE EXCEEDS CRITERIA	PERFORMANCE MEETS CRITERIA	HAS NOT MET PERFORMANCE CRITERIA	CANNOT JUDGE

Comments:

_____

_____

M-4.   The superintendent demonstrates effective organizational skills to achieve school, community, and district goals.

PERFORMANCE EXCEEDS CRITERIA	PERFORMANCE MEETS CRITERIA	HAS NOT MET PERFORMANCE CRITERIA	CANNOT JUDGE

Comments:

_____

_____

M-5.   The superintendent implements sound personnel procedures in recruiting, employing, and retaining the best qualified and most competent teachers, administrators, and other personnel.

PERFORMANCE EXCEEDS CRITERIA	PERFORMANCE MEETS CRITERIA	HAS NOT MET PERFORMANCE CRITERIA	CANNOT JUDGE

Comments:

_____

_____

M-6. The superintendent provides staff development for all categories of personnel consistent with individual needs, program evaluation results, and instructional improvement plans.

PERFORMANCE EXCEEDS CRITERIA	PERFORMANCE MEETS CRITERIA	HAS NOT MET PERFORMANCE CRITERIA	CANNOT JUDGE

Comments:

_____

_____

M-7. The superintendent plans and implements a systematic employee performance evaluation system.

PERFORMANCE EXCEEDS CRITERIA	PERFORMANCE MEETS CRITERIA	HAS NOT MET PERFORMANCE CRITERIA	CANNOT JUDGE

Comments:

_____

_____

■ Domain C: Communications and Community Relations

Performance Standards

C-1. The superintendent promotes effective communication and interpersonal relations within the school district.

PERFORMANCE EXCEEDS CRITERIA	PERFORMANCE MEETS CRITERIA	HAS NOT MET PERFORMANCE CRITERIA	CANNOT JUDGE

Comments:

_____

_____

C-2. The superintendent establishes and maintains effective channels of communication with board members and between the schools and community, strengthening support of constituencies and building coalitions.

PERFORMANCE EXCEEDS CRITERIA	PERFORMANCE MEETS CRITERIA	HAS NOT MET PERFORMANCE CRITERIA	CANNOT JUDGE

Comments:

_____

_____

C-3. The superintendent works collaboratively with staff, families, and community members to secure resources and to support the success of a diverse student population.

PERFORMANCE EXCEEDS CRITERIA	PERFORMANCE MEETS CRITERIA	HAS NOT MET PERFORMANCE CRITERIA	CANNOT JUDGE

Comments:

_____

_____

C-4. The superintendent creates an atmosphere of trust and mutual respect with staff and community.

PERFORMANCE EXCEEDS CRITERIA	PERFORMANCE MEETS CRITERIA	HAS NOT MET PERFORMANCE CRITERIA	CANNOT JUDGE

Comments:

_____

_____

■ Domain P: Professionalism

Performance Standards

P-1. The superintendent models professional, moral, and ethical standards as well as personal integrity in all interactions.

PERFORMANCE EXCEEDS CRITERIA	PERFORMANCE MEETS CRITERIA	HAS NOT MET PERFORMANCE CRITERIA	CANNOT JUDGE

Comments:

_____

_____

P-2. The superintendent works in a collegial and collaborative manner with school personnel and the community to promote and support the mission and goals of the school district.

PERFORMANCE EXCEEDS CRITERIA	PERFORMANCE MEETS CRITERIA	HAS NOT MET PERFORMANCE CRITERIA	CANNOT JUDGE

Comments:

_____

_____

P-3. The superintendent takes responsibility for and participates in a meaningful and continuous process of professional development that results in the enhancement of student learning.

PERFORMANCE EXCEEDS CRITERIA	PERFORMANCE MEETS CRITERIA	HAS NOT MET PERFORMANCE CRITERIA	CANNOT JUDGE

Comments:

_____

_____

P-4. The superintendent provides service to the profession, the district, and the community.

PERFORMANCE EXCEEDS CRITERIA	PERFORMANCE MEETS CRITERIA	HAS NOT MET PERFORMANCE CRITERIA	CANNOT JUDGE

Comments:

_____

_____

■ Evaluation Summary ■

■ Strengths

■ Areas for Improvement

Signatures:

_____   _____
Superintendent   School Board Chair

_____   _____
Date   Date

SUPERINTENDENT'S SIGNATURE ACKNOWLEDGES RECEIPT OF THIS FORM.
WRITTEN COMMENTS MAY BE ATTACHED.
COMMENTS ATTACHED: ____ YES ____ NO

Appendix H

SAMPLE
SUMMATIVE EVALUATION FORM II

■ 4-level rating scale (7 pages) ■

Superintendent Summative Evaluation

Superintendent's Name _____

Evaluator _____

Academic/Fiscal Year _____

<u>DIRECTIONS</u>

To be completed by the School Board as documentation of the superintendent's annual evaluation.

■ Domain G: Policy and Governance

Performance Standards	Performance Exceeds Criteria	Performance Meets Criteria	Performance Requires Improvement	Performance Is Unsatisfactory	Cannot Judge
G-1 The superintendent works with the school board to develop and implement policies that define organizational expectations.					
G-2 The superintendent functions as the primary instructional leader for the school district, relying on support from staff as necessary when advising the school board.					
G-3 The superintendent oversees the administration of the school district's day-to-day operations.					
G-4 The superintendent works with all individuals, groups, agencies, committees, and organizations to provide and maintain schools that are safe and productive.					

Comments _____

_____

_____

_____

_____

_____

_____

_____

_____

_____

_____

■ Domain A: Planning and Assessment

Performance Standards	Performance Exceeds Criteria	Performance Meets Criteria	Performance Requires Improvement	Performance Is Unsatisfactory	Cannot Judge
A-1 The superintendent effectively employs various processes for gathering, analyzing, and using data for decision making.					
A-2 The superintendent organizes the collaborative development and implementation of a district strategic plan based on analysis of data from a variety of sources.					
A-3 The superintendent plans, implements, supports, and assesses instructional programs that enhance teaching and student achievement of the state educational standards.					
A-4 The superintendent develops plans for effective allocation of fiscal and other resources.					

Comments

■ Domain L: Instructional Leadership

Performance Standards	Performance Exceeds Criteria	Performance Meets Criteria	Performance Requires Improvement	Performance Is Unsatisfactory	Cannot Judge
L-1 The superintendent communicates a clear vision of excellence and continuous improvement consistent with the goals of the school district.					
L-2 The superintendent oversees the alignment, coordination, and delivery of assigned programs and/or curricular areas.					
L-3 The superintendent selects, inducts, supports, evaluates, and retains quality instructional and support personnel.					
L-4 The superintendent provides staff development programs consistent with the program evaluation results and school instructional improvement plans.					
L-5 The superintendent identifies, analyzes, and resolves problems using effective problem-solving techniques.					
L-6 The superintendent assesses factors affecting student achievement and serves as an agent of change for needed improvements.					

Comments

_____

_____

_____

_____

_____

_____

_____

_____

_____

_____

_____

■ Domain M: Organizational Management

Performance Standards	Performance Exceeds Criteria	Performance Meets Criteria	Performance Requires Improvement	Performance Is Unsatisfactory	Cannot Judge
M-1 The superintendent actively supports a safe and positive environment for students and staff.					
M-2 The superintendent develops procedures for working with the board of education that define mutual expectations, working relationships, and strategies for formulating district policies.					
M-3 The superintendent effectively manages human, material, and financial resources to ensure student learning and to comply with legal mandates.					
M-4 The superintendent demonstrates effective organizational skills to achieve school, community, and district goals.					
M-5 The superintendent implements sound personnel procedures in recruiting, employing, and retaining the best qualified and most competent teachers, administrators, and other personnel.					
M-6 The superintendent provides staff development for all categories of personnel consistent with individual needs, program evaluation results, and instructional improvement plans.					
M-7 The superintendent plans and implements a systematic employee performance evaluation system.					

Comments

■ Domain C: Communications and Community Relations

Performance Standards	Performance Exceeds Criteria	Performance Meets Criteria	Performance Requires Improvement	Performance Is Unsatisfactory	Cannot Judge
C-1 The superintendent promotes effective communication and interpersonal relations within the school district.					
C-2 The superintendent establishes and maintains effective channels of communication with board members and between the schools and community, strengthening support of constituencies and building coalitions.					
C-3 The superintendent works collaboratively with staff, families, and community members to secure resources and to support the success of a diverse student population.					
C-4 The superintendent creates an atmosphere of trust and mutual respect with staff and community.					

Comments
_____
_____
_____
_____
_____
_____
_____
_____
_____
_____
_____
_____
_____
_____
_____

■ Domain P: Professionalism

Performance Standards	Performance Exceeds Criteria	Performance Meets Criteria	Performance Requires Improvement	Performance Is Unsatisfactory	Cannot Judge
P-1 The superintendent models professional, moral, and ethical standards as well as personal integrity in all interactions.					
P-2 The superintendent works in a collegial and collaborative manner with school personnel and the community to promote and support the mission and goals of the school district.					
P-3 The superintendent takes responsibility for and participates in a meaningful and continuous process of professional development that results in the enhancement of student learning.					
P-4 The superintendent provides service to the profession, the district, and the community.					

Comments

■ Evaluation Summary ■

■ Strengths

■ Areas for Improvement

Signatures:

_____	_____
Superintendent	School Board Chair
_____	_____
Date	Date

SUPERINTENDENT'S SIGNATURE ACKNOWLEDGES RECEIPT OF THIS FORM.
WRITTEN COMMENTS MAY BE ATTACHED.
COMMENTS ATTACHED: ____ YES   ____ NO

■ 3-level rating scale (4 pages) ■

Superintendent Summative Evaluation

Superintendent's Name _____

Evaluator _____

Academic/Fiscal Year _____

<u>DIRECTIONS</u>

To be completed by the School Board as documentation of the superintendent's evaluation.

Domain G: Policy and Governance Performance Standards	Performance Exceeds Criteria	Performance Meets Criteria	Has Not Met Performance Criteria	Cannot Judge
G-1. The superintendent works with the school board to develop and implement policies that define organizational expectations.				
G-2. The superintendent functions as the primary instructional leader for the school district, relying on support from staff as necessary when advising the school board.				
G-3. The superintendent oversees the administration of the school district's day-to-day operations.				
G-4. The superintendent works with all individuals, groups, agencies, committees, and organizations to provide and maintain schools that are safe and productive.				
Domain A: Planning and Assessment Performance Standards				
A-1. The superintendent effectively employs various processes for gathering, analyzing, and using data for decision making.				
A-2. The superintendent organizes the collaborative development and implementation of a district strategic plan based on analysis of data from a variety of sources.				
A-3. The superintendent plans, implements, supports, and assesses instructional programs that enhance teaching and student achievement of the state educational standards.				
A-4. The superintendent develops plans for effective allocation of fiscal and other resources.				

Domain L: Instructional Leadership Performance Standards	Performance Exceeds Criteria	Performance Meets Criteria	Has Not Met Performance Criteria	Cannot Judge
L-1. The superintendent communicates a clear vision of excellence and continuous improvement consistent with the goals of the school district.				
L-2. The superintendent oversees the alignment, coordination, and delivery of assigned programs and/or curricular areas.				
L-3. The superintendent selects, inducts, supports, evaluates, and retains quality instructional and support personnel.				
L-4. The superintendent provides staff development programs consistent with the program evaluation results and school instructional improvement plans.				
L-5. The superintendent identifies, analyzes, and resolves problems using effective problem-solving techniques.				
L-6. The superintendent assesses factors affecting student achievement and serves as an agent of change for needed improvements.				
Domain M: Organizational Management Performance Standards				
M-1. The superintendent actively supports a safe and positive environment for students and staff.				
M-2. The superintendent develops procedures for working with the board of education that define mutual expectations, working relationships, and strategies for formulating district policies.				
M-3. The superintendent effectively manages human, material, and financial resources to ensure student learning and to comply with legal mandates.				
M-4. The superintendent demonstrates effective organizational skills to achieve school, community, and district goals.				
M-5. The superintendent implements sound personnel procedures in recruiting, employing, and retaining the best qualified and most competent teachers, administrators, and other personnel.				
M-6. The superintendent provides staff development for all categories of personnel consistent with individual needs, program evaluation results, and instructional improvement plans.				
M-7. The superintendent plans and implements a systematic employee performance evaluation system.				

Domain C: Communications & Community Relations Performance Standards	Performance Exceeds Criteria	Performance Meets Criteria	Has Not Met Performance Criteria	Cannot Judge
C-1. The superintendent promotes effective communication and interpersonal relations within the school district.				
C-2. The superintendent establishes and maintains effective channels of communication with board members and between the schools and community, strengthening support of constituencies and building coalitions.				
C-3. The superintendent works collaboratively with staff, families, and community members to secure resources and to support the success of a diverse student population.				
C-4. The superintendent creates an atmosphere of trust and mutual respect with staff and community.				
Domain P: Professionalism Performance Standards				
P-1. The superintendent models professional, moral, and ethical standards as well as personal integrity in all interactions.				
P-2. The superintendent works in a collegial and collaborative manner with school personnel and the community to promote and support the mission and goals of the school district.				
P-3. The superintendent takes responsibility for and participates in a meaningful and continuous process of professional development that results in the enhancement of student learning.				
P-4. The superintendent provides service to the profession, the district, and the community.				

Comments

_____

_____

_____

_____

_____

_____

■ **Evaluation Summary** ■

■ **Strengths**

■ **Areas for Improvement**

Signatures:

_____   _____
Superintendent   School Board Chair

_____   _____
Date   Date

SUPERINTENDENT'S SIGNATURE ACKNOWLEDGES RECEIPT OF THIS FORM.
WRITTEN COMMENTS MAY BE ATTACHED.
COMMENTS ATTACHED: ____ YES ____ NO

Appendix I

SAMPLE
SUMMATIVE EVALUATION FORM III

■ 4-level rating scale (7 pages) ■

Superintendent Summative Evaluation

_____   _____
              Superintendent   Academic Year

Directions: The evaluation is to be completed by the School Board as documentation of the
              superintendent's annual evaluation. Based upon evidence gathered through
              appropriate sources, select the rating for each job responsibility that most closely
              describes the superintendent's performance. Add comments where appropriate.

Domain G: POLICY & GOVERNANCE	Exceeds Expectations	Meets Expectations	Needs Assistance	Unsatisfactory
Performance Standards				
G-1 The superintendent works with the school board to develop and implement policies that define organizational expectations.	☐	☐	☐	☐
G-2 The superintendent functions as the primary instructional leader for the school district, relying on support from staff as necessary when advising the school board.	☐	☐	☐	☐
G-3 The superintendent oversees the administration of the school district's day-to-day operations.	☐	☐	☐	☐
G-4 The superintendent works with all individuals, groups, agencies, committees, and organizations to provide and maintain schools that are safe and productive.	☐	☐	☐	☐

Comments: _____

_____

_____

_____

_____

Domain A: PLANNING & ASSESSMENT	Exceeds Expectations	Meets Expectations	Needs Assistance	Unsatisfactory
Performance Standards				
A-1 The superintendent effectively employs various processes for gathering, analyzing, and using data for decision making.	☐	☐	☐	☐
A-2 The superintendent organizes the collaborative development and implementation of a district strategic plan based on analysis of data from a variety of sources.	☐	☐	☐	☐
A-3 The superintendent plans, implements, supports, and assesses instructional programs that enhance teaching and student achievement of the state educational standards.	☐	☐	☐	☐
A-4 The superintendent develops plans for effective allocation of fiscal and other resources.	☐	☐	☐	☐

Comments: _____

_____

_____

_____

_____

_____

_____

_____

_____

_____

_____

_____

_____

_____

Domain L: **INSTRUCTIONAL LEADERSHIP**	**Exceeds Expectations**	**Meets Expectations**	**Needs Assistance**	**Unsatisfactory**
Performance Standards				
L-1 The superintendent communicates a clear vision of excellence and continuous improvement consistent with the goals of the school district.	☐	☐	☐	☐
L-2 The superintendent oversees the alignment, coordination, and delivery of assigned programs and/or curricular areas.	☐	☐	☐	☐
L-3 The superintendent selects, inducts, supports, evaluates, and retains quality instructional and support personnel.	☐	☐	☐	☐
L-4 The superintendent provides staff development programs consistent with program evaluation results and school instructional improvement plans.	☐	☐	☐	☐
L-5 The superintendent identifies, analyzes, and resolves problems using effective problem-solving techniques.	☐	☐	☐	☐
L-6 The superintendent assesses factors affecting student achievement and serves as an agent of change for needed improvements.	☐	☐	☐	☐

Comments: _____

_____

_____

_____

_____

_____

Domain M:
ORGANIZATIONAL MANAGEMENT

	Exceeds Expectations	Meets Expectations	Needs Assistance	Unsatisfactory
Performance Standards				
M-1 The superintendent actively supports a safe and positive environment for students and staff.	☐	☐	☐	☐
M-2 The superintendent develops procedures for working with the board of education that define mutual expectations, working relationships, and strategies for formulating district policies.	☐	☐	☐	☐
M-3 The superintendent effectively manages human, material, and financial resources to ensure student learning and to comply with legal mandates.	☐	☐	☐	☐
M-4 The superintendent demonstrates effective organizational skills to achieve school, community, and district goals.	☐	☐	☐	☐
M-5 The superintendent implements sound personnel procedures in recruiting, employing, and retaining the best qualified and most competent teachers, administrators, and other personnel.	☐	☐	☐	☐
M-6 The superintendent provides staff development for all categories of personnel consistent with individual needs, program evaluation results, and instructional improvement plans.	☐	☐	☐	☐
M-7 The superintendent plans and implements a systematic employee performance evaluation system.	☐	☐	☐	☐

Comments: _____

Domain C: COMMUNICATIONS & COMMUNITY RELATIONS	Exceeds Expectations	Meets Expectations	Needs Assistance	Unsatisfactory
Performance Standards				
C-1 The superintendent promotes effective communication and interpersonal relations within the school district.	☐	☐	☐	☐
C-2 The superintendent establishes and maintains effective channels of communication with board members and between the schools and community, strengthening support of constituencies and building coalitions.	☐	☐	☐	☐
C-3 The superintendent works collaboratively with staff, families, and community members to secure resources and to support the success of a diverse student population.	☐	☐	☐	☐
C-4 The superintendent creates an atmosphere of trust and mutual respect with staff and community.	☐	☐	☐	☐

Comments: _____

_____

_____

_____

_____

_____

_____

_____

_____

_____

_____

Domain P: PROFESSIONALISM	Exceeds Expectations	Meets Expectations	Needs Assistance	Unsatisfactory
Performance Standards				
P-1 The superintendent models professional, moral, and ethical standards as well as personal integrity in all interactions.	☐	☐	☐	☐
P-2 The superintendent works in a collegial and collaborative manner with school personnel and the community to promote and support the mission and goals of the school district.	☐	☐	☐	☐
P-3 The superintendent takes responsibility for and participates in a meaningful and continuous process of professional development that results in the enhancement of student learning.	☐	☐	☐	☐
P-4 The superintendent provides service to the profession, the district, and the community.	☐	☐	☐	☐

Comments: _____

_____

_____

_____

_____

_____

_____

_____

_____

_____

_____

_____

Strengths

Areas for Continuous Improvement

Board Member Signatures

_____   _____

_____   _____

_____   Date: _____

Superintendent Signature*

_____   Date: _____

_____

*Written comments may be attached. If comments are attached, initial and date here. _____

■ 3-level rating scale (4 pages) ■

Superintendent Summative Evaluation

_____   _____
Superintendent   Academic Year

Directions: The evaluation is to be completed by the School Board as documentation of the
              superintendent's annual evaluation. Based upon evidence gathered through
              appropriate sources, select the rating for each job responsibility that most closely
              describes the superintendent's performance. Add comments where appropriate.

Domain G: POLICY & GOVERNANCE _Performance Standards_	Exceeds Expectations	Meets Expectations	Has Not Met Expectations
G-1 The superintendent works with the school board to develop and implement policies that define organizational expectations.	☐	☐	☐
G-2 The superintendent functions as the primary instructional leader for the school district, relying on support from staff as necessary when advising the school board.	☐	☐	☐
G-3 The superintendent oversees the administration of the school district's day-to-day operations.	☐	☐	☐
G-4 The superintendent works with all individuals, groups, agencies, committees, and organizations to provide and maintain schools that are safe and productive.	☐	☐	☐
Domain A: PLANNING & ASSESSMENT _Performance Standards_			
A-1 The superintendent effectively employs various processes for gathering, analyzing, and using data for decision making.	☐	☐	☐
A-2 The superintendent organizes the collaborative development and implementation of a district strategic plan based on analysis of data from a variety of sources.	☐	☐	☐
A-3 The superintendent plans, implements, supports, and assesses instructional programs that enhance teaching and student achievement of the state educational standards.	☐	☐	☐
A-4 The superintendent develops plans for effective allocation of fiscal and other resources.	☐	☐	☐

Domain L: INSTRUCTIONAL LEADERSHIP *Performance Standards*	Exceeds Expectations	Meets Expectations	Has Not Met Expectations
L-1 The superintendent communicates a clear vision of excellence and continuous improvement consistent with the goals of the school district.	☐	☐	☐
L-2 The superintendent oversees the alignment, coordination, and delivery of assigned programs and/or curricular areas.	☐	☐	☐
L-3 The superintendent selects, inducts, supports, evaluates, and retains quality instructional and support personnel.	☐	☐	☐
L-4 The superintendent provides staff development programs consistent with program evaluation results and school instructional improvement plans.	☐	☐	☐
L-5. The superintendent identifies, analyzes, and resolves problems using effective problem-solving techniques.	☐	☐	☐
L-6. The superintendent assesses factors affecting studentachievement and serves as an agent of change for needed improvements.	☐	☐	☐

Domain M: ORGANIZATIONAL MANAGEMENT *Performance Standards*			
M-1 The superintendent actively supports a safe and positive environment for students and staff.	☐	☐	☐
M-2 The superintendent develops procedures for working with the board of education that define mutual expectations, working relationships, and strategies for formulating district policies.	☐	☐	☐
M-3 The superintendent effectively manages human, material, and financial resources to ensure student learning and to comply with legal mandates.	☐	☐	☐
M-4 The superintendent demonstrates effective organizational skills to achieve school, community, and district goals.	☐	☐	☐
M-5. The superintendent implements sound personnel procedures in recruiting, employing, and retaining the best qualified and most competent teachers, administrators, and other personnel.	☐	☐	☐
M-6. The superintendent provides staff development for all categories of personnel consistent with individual needs, program evaluation results, and instructional improvement plans.	☐	☐	☐
M-7. The superintendent plans and implements a systematic employee performance evaluation system.	☐	☐	☐

Domain C: COMMUNICATIONS & COMMUNITY RELATIONS

Performance Standards

	Exceeds Expectations	Meets Expectations	Has Not Met Expectations
C-1 The superintendent promotes effective communication and interpersonal relations within the school district.	☐	☐	☐
C-2 The superintendent establishes and maintains effective channels of communication with board members and between the schools and community, strengthening support of constituencies and building coalitions.	☐	☐	☐
C-3 The superintendent works collaboratively with staff, families, and community members to secure resources and to support the success of a diverse student population.	☐	☐	☐
C-4 The superintendent creates an atmosphere of trust and mutual respect with staff and community.	☐	☐	☐

Domain P: PROFESSIONALISM

Performance Standards

P-1 The superintendent models professional, moral, and ethical standards as well as personal integrity in all interactions.	☐	☐	☐
P-2 The superintendent works in a collegial and collaborative manner with school personnel and the community to promote and support the mission and goals of the school district.	☐	☐	☐
P-3 The superintendent takes responsibility for and participates in a meaningful and continuous process of professional development that results in theenhancement of student learning.	☐	☐	☐
P-4 The superintendent provides service to the profession, the district, and the community.	☐	☐	☐

Notes

_____

_____

_____

_____

_____

_____

_____

_____

<u>Strengths</u>

<u>Areas for Continuous Improvement</u>

<u>Board Member Signatures</u>

_____   _____

_____   _____

_____   Date: _____

<u>Superintendent Signature</u> *

_____   Date: _____

_____

* Written comments may be attached. If comments are attached, initial and date here. _____

Appendix J

SAMPLE
SUMMATIVE EVALUATION FORM IV

■ 4-level rating scale (3 pages) ■

Superintendent Summative Evaluation

_____   _____
Superintendent   Academic Year

Directions: The evaluation is to be completed by the School Board as documentation of the
superintendent's annual evaluation. Based upon evidence gathered through
appropriate sources, select the rating for each job responsibility that most closely
describes the superintendent's performance. Add comments where appropriate.

Domain G: POLICY AND GOVERNANCE	Exceeds Expectations	Meets Expectations	Needs Assistance	Unsatisfactory
	☐	☐	☐	☐

Comments: _____

_____

_____

_____

_____

_____

Domain A: PLANNING AND ASSESSMENT	Exceeds Expectations	Meets Expectations	Needs Assistance	Unsatisfactory
	☐	☐	☐	☐

Comments: _____

_____

_____

_____

_____

_____

_____

_____

Domain L: INSTRUCTIONAL LEADERSHIP	Exceeds Expectations	Meets Expectations	Needs Assistance	Unsatisfactory
	☐	☐	☐	☐

Comments: _____

_____

_____

_____

_____

_____

_____

Domain M: ORGANIZATIONAL MANAGEMENT	Exceeds Expectations	Meets Expectations	Needs Assistance	Unsatisfactory
	☐	☐	☐	☐

Comments: _____

_____

_____

_____

_____

_____

_____

Domain C: COMMUNICATIONS AND COMMUNITY RELATIONS	Exceeds Expectations	Meets Expectations	Needs Assistance	Unsatisfactory
	☐	☐	☐	☐

Comments: _____

_____

_____

_____

_____

_____

_____

Domain P: PROFESSIONALISM	Exceeds Expectations	Meets Expectations	Needs Assistance	Unsatisfactory
	☐	☐	☐	☐

Comments: _____

_____

_____

_____

_____

_____

_____

Strengths

Areas for Continuous Improvement

Board Member Signatures

_____   _____

_____   _____

_____   Date: _____

Superintendent Signature[1]

_____   Date: _____

---

[1] Written comments may be attached. If comments are attached, initial and date here. _____

■ 3-level rating scale (3 pages) ■

Superintendent Summative Evaluation

_____   _____
            Superintendent   Academic Year

Directions: The evaluation is to be completed by the School Board as documentation of the
              superintendent's annual evaluation. Based upon evidence gathered through
              appropriate sources, select the rating for each job responsibility that most closely
              describes the superintendent's performance. Add comments where appropriate.

Domain G: **POLICY AND GOVERNANCE**	**Exceeds Expectations**	**Meets Expectations**	**Has Not Met Expectations**
	☐	☐	☐

Comments: _____

_____

_____

_____

_____

_____

_____

_____

Domain A: **PLANNING AND ASSESSMENT**	**Exceeds Expectations**	**Meets Expectations**	**Has Not Met Expectations**
	☐	☐	☐

Comments: _____

_____

_____

_____

_____

_____

_____

_____

_____

Domain L: **INSTRUCTIONAL** **LEADERSHIP**	**Exceeds** Expectations ☐	**Meets** Expectations ☐	**Has Not Met** Expectations ☐

Comments: _____

_____

_____

_____

_____

_____

_____

Domain M: **ORGANIZATIONAL** **MANAGEMENT**	**Exceeds** Expectations ☐	**Meets** Expectations ☐	**Has Not Met** Expectations ☐

Comments: _____

_____

_____

_____

_____

_____

_____

Domain C: **COMMUNICATIONS** **AND COMMUNITY** **RELATIONS**	**Exceeds** Expectations ☐	**Meets** Expectations ☐	**Has Not Met** Expectations ☐

Comments: _____

_____

_____

_____

_____

_____

_____

Domain P: PROFESSIONALISM	Exceeds Expectations	Meets Expectations	Has Not Met Expectations
	☐	☐	☐

Comments: _____

_____

_____

_____

_____

_____

_____

Strengths

Areas for Continuous Improvement

Board Member Signatures

_____   _____

_____   _____

_____   Date: _____

Superintendent Signature*

_____   Date: _____

_____

* Written comments may be attached. If comments are attached, initial and date here. _____

Appendix K

SAMPLE
BOARD OF EDUCATION POLICY—
EVALUATION OF THE
SUPERINTENDENT

The Board of Education will evaluate the performance of the superintendent annually in order to assist both the Board and superintendent in the proper discharge of their responsibilities and enable the Board to provide the district with the best possible leadership.

Through the evaluation of the superintendent the board strives to achieve these objectives:

- clarify for the superintendent his or her role in the district as understood by the Board;
- clarify for individual board members the role of superintendent in light of her or his responsibilities, authority, and organizational expectations;
- develop a unity of purpose in order to achieve high-priority goals and objectives;
- develop an opportunity for goal achievement through regular appraisal and feedback;
- assist the superintendent in professional development;
- improve the quality of education for the pupils of this district; and
- enhance the organizational climate through the involvement and growth of individuals.

The Board may choose to be advised or assisted in the process by a consultant. The evaluation shall be based on the performance expectations as detailed in the job description of the position of superintendent. The job description and any revisions thereof shall be developed in consultation with the superintendent and adopted by the board.

EVALUATION PROCESS

Criteria used to evaluate the superintendent will be based on the job description of the superintendent. The major areas (domains) of responsibility of the superintendent, performance expectations (standards) in each domain, and behavioral indicators of each performance expectation pursuant to the job description are specified in the accompanying policy, *Duties of the Superintendent*. The evaluation shall focus on the performance expectations as well as the achievement of the superintendent's annual goal(s). It shall be based on valid and reliable data sources, including direct observation, goal attainment, gains in student achievement, client surveys, and other appropriate indicators of performance. Survey forms, goal forms, and other forms developed for use in the process are detailed in the *Procedures Governing Superintendent Evaluation*. The board will provide both interim and summative evaluations on the respective forms designed and adopted for this process.

ANNUAL GOAL(S)

The superintendent, in conjunction with the Board, will set annual goals for improvement that are congruent with the system's goals. A plan for goal achievement will be developed and will include a schedule for goal attainment with indicators of interim progress. The goal(s) will be reviewed and adjusted as necessary. The superintendent will report progress on achieving the goal(s) at regularly scheduled intervals throughout the evaluation process. Indicators of goal attainment include documentation via the superintendent's oral and written reports and other materials.

EVALUATION CONFERENCES

Quarterly conferences between the superintendent and Board will be scheduled in order to provide continuity and enhance communication during the process of evaluation. Conferences will be scheduled as agenda items for closed executive sessions, unless the superintendent requests that they be held in public, in accordance with the following schedule:

By

September 1 Superintendent meets with Board to jointly set her or his annual goal(s).

November 15 Superintendent meets with Board to discuss progress made on goal attainment and receives feedback on overall performance.

January 31 Superintendent meets with Board to discuss progress made on goal attainment and receives feedback on overall performance via an *Interim Review* document.

April 15 Superintendent meets with Board to discuss progress made on goal attainment and receive feedback on overall performance.

June 30 Superintendent meets with Board to discuss the annual *Summative Evaluation.*

The conferences shall include, but shall not be limited to, a review of the superintendent's performance based on the job description; a review of the superintendent's progress in goal achievement; and a review of appropriate indicators of student progress and growth.

The purpose of the annual summative conference is to provide a comprehensive review of the year's work, identify strategies for improvement and future goal setting, and recognize achievement and good professional practice. Adequate time will be allotted for the conference in order to address the required topics of discussion as well as to permit full exploration of solutions to any identified problems.

The Board president will sign the annual summative evaluation report at the time of the conference and the superintendent will sign it within five working days. The report will be filed in the superintendent's personnel file and a copy will be provided to the superintendent.

Reference to all applicable state laws/codes

Adopted: Date

Appendix L

SAMPLE
BOARD OF EDUCATION PROCEDURES
Evaluation of the Superintendent

Members of the Board of Education and superintendent will implement the following procedures:

1. The Board of Education and the superintendent shall jointly identify, in May of each school year, goals and priorities of the district for the coming year.
2. The Board of Education and the superintendent shall jointly identify, in June of each school year, the superintendent's personal goals, including student achievement goals, for the coming year.
3. The superintendent will develop an action plan for goal achievement. Each action plan will describe the major activities involved in achieving the objective, a timeline, and indicators of success.
4. By the end of July, the Board will review each plan and, after discussion, each plan will be approved, modified, or dropped. Upon approval, the superintendent will be required to implement the plans.
5. By the end of August, the Board and the superintendent will review the performance standards and evaluative instruments, the format for reviewing progress toward district goals, and the calendar of events that will lead to the completion of the evaluation.

6. By October 15, the superintendent is expected to provide the Board with a report on the progress being made on each goal at a scheduled closed-session meeting.

7. By January 1, the superintendent is expected to provide the board with a report on the progress being made on each goal at a scheduled closed-session meeting. At this time the Board will provide feedback to the superintendent in an *interim review* of progress.

8. By March 15, the superintendent is expected to provide the Board with a report on the progress being made on each goal at a scheduled closed-session meeting.

9. By April 30, the superintendent's performance, including goal achievement, will be assessed via a *summative evaluation* by the Board. A discussion between the superintendent and Board will provide an opportunity for the superintendent to provide an explanation for lack of goal achievement and for the Board to provide commendations if appropriate and suggestions for improvement.

10. Board members shall annually conduct a self-evaluation to determine the degree to which they are meeting their responsibilities as board members and the educational needs of the school community.

Adapted from New Jersey School Boards Association
   http://www.njsba.org/Field_Services/SR/policy.html

ADDITIONAL RESOURCES WITH ANNOTATIONS

Matrix of Resources on Superintendent Evaluation

Article	Conceptual Framework	Evaluation Development	Expectations	Other Personnel	School Board	State Sample	Student Achievement	Study	Superintendent Characteristics
Alabama Professional Education Personnel Evaluation Program (1997)	✓		✓		✓	✓			
Candoli, Cullen, & Stufflebeam (1997)	✓	✓	✓					✓	
Department of Public Instruction (NC) (1998)			✓			✓	✓		
Division of Teacher Education and Licensure, Virginia Department of Education (2000)	✓	✓	✓	✓	✓	✓			
Gemberling, Smith, & Villani (2000)			✓		✓		✓		
Glass, Bjork, & Brunner (2000)					✓			✓	✓
Goodman, Fullbright, & Zimmerman (1997)			✓		✓		✓	✓	
Illinois Association of School Boards (2002)		✓	✓		✓	✓			
Oregon School Board Association (1998)			✓			✓			
Technology Standards for School Administrators Collaborative (2001)			✓	✓					
Texas Association of School Administrators (1998)	✓					✓			

Alabama Professional Education Personnel Evaluation Program. (1997). *Board orientation manual for superintendent evaluation system*. Montgomery, AL: Alabama State Department of Education.

This document is intended for school board use. It provides competencies, indicators, and definitions for superintendents and a conceptual framework of the process. It also provides all forms for each step of the evaluation process as described in the document. Keywords: conceptual framework, expectations, school board, state sample.

Candoli, I. C., Cullen, K., & Stufflebeam, D. L. (1997). *Superintendent performance evaluation: Current practice and directions for improvement*. Norwell, MA: Kluwer Academic Press.

Section 1 of the book is an overview of the book itself. Section 2 describes the research methodology used in the study including descriptions of the composition of the research team and advisory panel, the method of working, the approach used to identify relevant materials and literature, the internal review process at CREATE for evaluating research products, and how the research findings were published and disseminated.

Section 3 provides a detailed description of the conceptual framework that guided the research. It begins with a discussion of the need for such research followed by the *AASA Professional Standards for the Superintendency* and a draft list of generic administrator duties. Finally, there is a detailed description of *The Personnel Evaluation Standards* developed by the Joint Committee on Standards of Educational Evaluation and the role they played in guiding this research.

Section 4 addresses the nature of the superintendency in the contemporary American school system. This section provides a useful framework for superintendents and school boards to develop and articulate a common view of the superintendency. Key research questions addressed in this section include:

- What is the history and evolution of the school district superintendency in the United States?
- What are the duties of the school district superintendent and what is the generic role?
- What does a typical superintendent job description look like?

Section 5 presents the findings of the research literature on the superintendent evaluation. This section describes the current status of superintendent performance evaluation and attempts to identify the most important issues and problems. Key questions discussed in this section include:

- How widespread is the practice of superintendent performance evaluation in the United States at the present time?
- How frequently do such evaluations take place?
- What are the purposes of superintendent performance evaluation?
- What are the criteria by which superintendents are evaluated?
- What methods or procedures are typically used?

Section 6 addresses these research questions:

- What alternative models are used to evaluate school district superintendents?
- What are the distinguishing features of these models, and what are their main strengths and weaknesses?

Section 7 addresses the question of what new models can be developed to improve existing models of superintendent evaluation. It includes a generic model built upon the strengths and weaknesses presented in section 6. Keywords: conceptual framework, evaluation development, expectations, study.

Department of Public Instruction. (1998). *Standards for superintendent evaluation.* Raleigh, NC: Department of Public Instruction (publications@dpi. state.nc.us).

This document reflects the indicators for evaluation of superintendents in the state of North Carolina. They are divided into five areas: vision; high student performance; safe and orderly schools; quality teachers, administrators, and staff; and effective and efficient operation. This document may be found electronically at http://www.dpi.state.nc.us/evalpsemployees/ suptstand.htm. Keywords: expectations, state sample, student achievement.

Division of Teacher Education and Licensure, Virginia Department of Education. (2000). *Guidelines for uniform performance standards and evaluation criteria for teachers, administrators, and superintendents.* Richmond, VA: Virginia Department of Education.

These guidelines provide the framework for school districts to develop criteria for teachers, administrators (including instructional, central office personnel, and principals), and superintendents. They are intended to provide guidance for school boards in the development of evaluation policies and procedures. Through these guidelines, the role and expectations of those individuals having the most effect on student learning and achievement will become clearer. They also provide continuity between the roles of teachers and administrators and their impact on student achievement. Recommendations for implementation, as well as performance indicators for teachers, adminis-trators, and superintendents, are included. Keywords: evaluation develop-ment, expectations, other personnel, school board, state sample, student achievement.

Gemberling, K. W., Smith, C. W., & Villani, J. S. (2000). *The keywork of school boards guidebook.* Alexandria, VA: National School Board Association.

This guidebook is intended to help school boards focus their efforts and un-derstanding on their key work, which is improving student achievement through community engagement. It focuses on eight key actions that success-ful school boards have attended to: vision, standards, assessment, accountabil-ity, resource alignment, climate, collaboration, and continuous improvement. Each of the key actions is outlined and discussed in a chapter of the guidebook.
  Each chapter includes

- a definition and an explanation of the key action;
- a self-assessment to gauge understanding and readiness;
- a list of questions for the board members, superintendent, and staff;
- an outline of roles and responsibilities of the superintendent and the board members;
- a series of considerations for planning purposes;
- an annotated bibliography of additional references including internet links; and
- a case study of an effective school board.

The purpose is to initiate and accelerate the development of an effective school board. Keywords: expectations, school board, student achievement.

Glass, T. E., Bjork, L., & Brunner, C. C. (2000). *The study of the American school superintendency 2000.* Arlington, VA: American Association of School Administrators.

This work reflects the findings of the American Association of School Adminis-trators (AASA) Ten-Year Study of the American School Superintendent. The re-sults were analyzed with an historical perspective when compared to the 1980 and 1990 data. The data are broken down into eight chapters. Chapter 1 de-scribes the superintendency and its future. Chapter 2 describes the study, its ob-jectives, population studied, content areas, the instrument used, sample selec-tion, implementation and return rate, and data analysis. Chapter 3 provides the personal characteristics of those studied. Chapter 4 is a snapshot of the profes-sional experience of the superintendents studied. Chapter 5 reflects the rela-tionship between the school board and the superintendent.

Chapters 6 and 7 focus on particular subsets of the sample population. Chapter 6 is a comprehensive description of female superintendents. Chapter 7 focuses on ethnic minority superintendents and provides similar data.

Chapter 8 paints a picture of the professional preparation and training of school superintendents. It looks at quantity as well as quality of this training. Keywords: school board, study, superintendent characteristics.

Goodman, R. H., Fullbright, L., & Zimmerman, W. G. Jr. (1997). *Getting there from here—School board–superintendent collaboration: Creating a school governance team capable of raising student achievement.* Arlington, VA: New England School Development Council and Educational Research Service.

This publication reflects the findings of the New England School Development Council's (NESDEC) year-long national study focused on school board–superintendent collaboration for higher student achievement. The core of the research was field-oriented one-on-one interviews with 130 educators, parents, and other citizens in 10 diverse school districts in five states.

Part One: "What the Study Found in Five States" summarizes the findings of these interviews. Part Two: "Recommendations for Creating a School Governance Team Capable of Raising Student Achievement" outlines three major goals and six steps to success in high-performance governance teams.

The three major goals are:

• Do what is necessary to provide effective and stable leadership among school boards and superintendents of schools.
• Ensure that there is a clear understanding and upholding of the respective roles and responsibilities of board members and superintendents.
• Support a high degree of collaboration between each school board and its superintendent, who together must view themselves as the "school district governance team for higher student achievement."

The six steps to success are:

• Build a foundation for teamwork.
• Get the best and most capable team players.
• Ensure that the team players know their roles and responsibilities.
• Get into team training.
• Adopt good team strategies.
• Convince others to support the team.

These recommendations are not intended to be all-inclusive. Keywords: expectations, school board, student achievement, study.

Illinois Association of School Boards. (2002). *How to develop a performance evaluation process.* Springfield: Illinois Association of School Boards.

The Illinois Association of School Boards presents an eight-step checklist by which a superintendent evaluation process may be established. The purpose is not to produce an evaluation. Rather, the aim is to establish a *process* for effective evaluation. The focus suggests that the emphasis is on the future rather than the past.

This guide could be useful to school boards who have not yet established such a process as well as those who need to modify existing processes to accommodate academic improvement goals. The eight steps include:

- Develop a focus on performance.
- Review existing documents.
- Agree on expectations.
- Examine School Board performance.
- Get it in writing.
- Report progress.
- Evaluate performance.
- Focus on the future.

In addition, the guide provides explanatory information on the steps listed above, legal references to the Illinois school code, a model for evaluating the superintendent, a timeline for the process, and an appendix of additional resources. Keywords: evaluation development, expectations, school board, state sample.

Oregon School Board Association. (1998). *Evaluating superintendents.* Salem, OR: Oregon School Board Association.

This document provides a rationale for superintendent evaluation and description of how and when this evaluation should be done. The remainder of the document is an evaluation form on which superintendents are rated in areas of leadership and district culture, policy and governance, communications and community relations, organizational management, curriculum planning and development, instructional leadership, human resources leadership, values and ethics of leadership, labor relations, and district goals. It is retrievable electronically at http://www.orlocalgov.org/osba by selecting "OSBA Services," "Leadership," and then downloading "Superintendent Evaluation." Keywords: expectations, state sample.

Technology Standards for School Administrators (TSSA) Collaborative. (2001). *Technology standards for school administrators.* Naperville, IL: North Central Regional Technology in Education Consortium.

This publication is a consensus among educational stakeholders of what best indicates accomplished school leadership for comprehensive and effective use of technology in schools. The assumption is that administrators should be competent users of information and the tools of the information age. The standards reflect the knowledge and skills that are the core for any administrator regardless of specific job role. These standards are then extended to specific job roles that include superintendent and executive cabinet, district-level leaders, and campus-level leaders.

The standards are presented as six statements with corresponding sets of competencies. The six standards are

- Leadership and vision;
- Learning and teaching;
- Productivity and professional development;
- Support, management, and operations;
- Assessment and evaluation; and
- Social, legal, and ethical issues.

In addition, the standards include illustrative vignettes of administrator use of technology. Keywords: expectations, other personnel.

Texas Association of School Administrators. (1998). *Superintendent evaluation handbook.* Austin, TX: Texas Association of School Administrators.

This document describes a systematic process for developing, revising, and administering a process of superintendent evaluation. It includes research findings specific to superintendent evaluation as well as recommendations for practice provided by experienced superintendents and the Texas Association of School Administrators' (TASA) general council. Several sample appraisals are included in the appendix. Throughout the handbook, a performance-based approach is emphasized, but the handbook also includes other types of traditional instrumentation. Keywords: evaluation development, state sample.

INDEX

ABOUT THE AUTHORS

Michael F. DiPaola joined the faculty of the educational policy, planning, and leadership program for the School of Education at The College of William and Mary in August 1998. His career in public education has spanned three decades, including a decade of classroom teaching. He also served as an assistant principal in a 7–12 building and as principal of a grade 10–12 senior high school. Prior to joining the faculty at the college, Dr. DiPaola was the superintendent of the public schools in Pitman, New Jersey, for six years. He earned his doctorate in educational administration from Rutgers, The State University of New Jersey.

His teaching and research interests include school leadership, the interactions of professionals in school organizations, performance evaluation, intraorganizational conflict, professional preparation of administrators, the principalship, and the superintendency. With colleagues, he developed Virginia's uniform performance standards and evaluation criteria and he has worked with many school districts and state and national educational organizations to design and develop evaluation systems for teachers, administrators, superintendents, and support personnel. He is currently working with the American Association of School Administrators to develop training programs for superintendent evaluation. Dr. DiPaola's latest publications include the chapters "Change and conflict: Daily challenges for school leaders" in *Leadership and effective education*, edited by N. Bennett, M. P. Crawford, and M. Cartwright, and, with C. Walther-Thomas, "What instructional leaders need to know about special education" in *Best practices, best thinking, and emerging issues in school leadership*, edited by W. Owings and L. Kaplan.

James H. Stronge is Heritage Professor of educational policy, planning, and leadership in the School of Education at The College of William and Mary in Williamsburg, Virginia. He received his doctorate, in the area of educational administration and planning, from the University of Alabama. He has been a teacher, counselor, and district-level administrator, and among his primary research interests are teacher effectiveness, student success, and teacher and administrator performance evaluation. Dr. Stronge has worked with numerous school districts and state and national educational organizations to design and develop evaluation systems for teachers, administrators, superintendents, and support personnel. He is currently working with the American Association of School Administrators to develop training programs in superintendent evaluation. His most recent research project, in conjunction with SERVE (the regional educational laboratory located at the University of North Carolina, Greensboro) and various school districts, explores the connection between teacher effectiveness and student achievement.

Dr. Stronge is the author and coauthor of numerous articles, books, and technical reports on teacher, administrator, and support personnel evaluation. Selected authored or edited publications include *Evaluating professional support personnel in education* (Sage Publications), *Evaluation handbook for professional support personnel* (Center for Research on Educational Accountability and Teacher Evaluation), *Evaluating teaching: A guide to current thinking and best practice* (Corwin Press), *Teacher evaluation and student achievement* (National Education Association), and *Handbook on teacher portfolios for evaluation and professional development* (Eye-on-Education). Most recently, he has written the book *Qualities of effective teaching*, for the Association for Supervision and Curriculum Development (July, 2002).